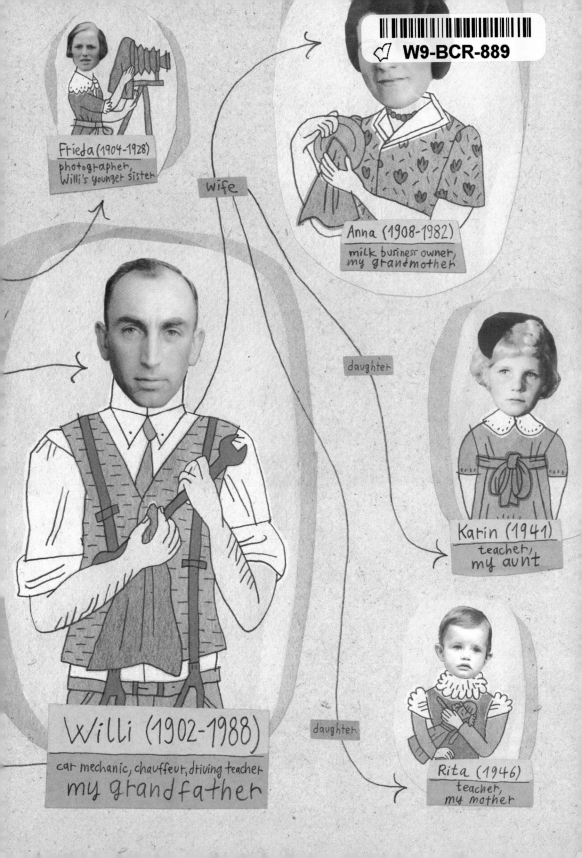

Frieda (1904-1928)
photographer,
Willi's younger sister

wife

Anna (1908-1982)
milk business owner,
my grandmother

daughter

Karin (1941)
teacher,
my aunt

Willi (1902-1988)
car mechanic, chauffeur, driving teacher
my grandfather

daughter

Rita (1946)
teacher,
my mother

# BELONGING

## A German Reckons with History and Home

NORA KRUG

SCRIBNER

New York   London   Toronto   Sydney   New Delhi

Scribner
An Imprint of Simon & Schuster, Inc.
1230 Avenue of the Americas
New York, NY 10020

First Scribner trade paperback edition September 2019

SCRIBNER and design are registered trademarks of The Gale Group, Inc.,
used under license by Simon & Schuster, Inc., the publisher of this work.

For information about special discounts for bulk purchases,
please contact Simon & Schuster Special Sales at 1-866-506-1949
or business@simonandschuster.com.

The Simon & Schuster Speakers Bureau can bring authors to your live event.
For more information or to book an event, contact the Simon & Schuster Speakers Bureau
at 1-866-248-3049 or visit our website at www.simonspeakers.com.

Manufactured in the United States of America

5  7  9  10  8  6

Library of Congress Cataloging-in-Publication Data is available.

ISBN 978-1-4767-9662-8
ISBN 978-1-4767-9663-5 (pbk)
ISBN 978-1-4767-9664-2 (ebook)

To my old family
and my new family

Ort

Name

Nr.

Jahrgang

Bestellnummer 9951/2

Hansaplast is a brand of bandage developed in 1922. My mother applied it to my bleeding knee after a roller-skating accident when I was six years old. Next to my mother, Hansaplast was the safest thing in the world. No matter if your skin is thick or thin, smooth or wrinkly, dry or moist, Hansaplast is so reliable that it won't come off until your wound has fully healed. It is the most tenacious bandage on the planet, and it hurts when you tear it off to look at your scar.

I was standing on the rooftop of my friend's apartment
building — the only person I knew so far in the city.
I had just moved here from Berlin to study.
I didn't know anyone. No one knew me.

Everything was possible.

An elderly woman sitting in a lounge chair
had overheard our conversation.

"Where are you from?" she asked me.
"I'm from Germany."

"That's what I thought."

"Have you ever been to Germany?" I asked.
"Yes. A long, long time ago."
She avoided eye contact.

And then I understood.

She went on to tell me about how she had survived the concentration camp because one of the female guards had rescued her from the gas chamber sixteen times at the last moment.

The guard, who had exhibited merciless violence toward everyone else in the camp, regularly knocking prisoners' heads together for punishment, had had, the elderly woman suspected, a secret crush on her.

F E M A L E

16 times on the edge of the gas chamber.

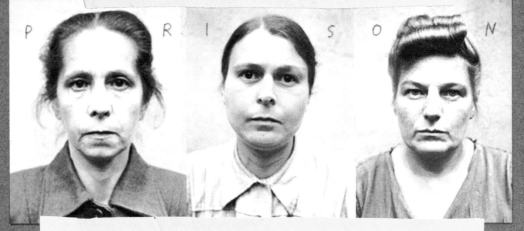

P R I S O N

16 times escaping immediate death by a hairsbreadth.

G U A R D S

16 times seeing others walk to their deaths while you must live.

A familiar heat began to form in the pit of my stomach.

How do you react, as a German, standing across from
a human being who reveals this memory to you?

I remained silent.

"That was a long time ago," she finally said.
"I'm sure things have changed. You seem like someone
who was raised by loving parents."

I nodded.

# 1.
# EARLY DAWNING

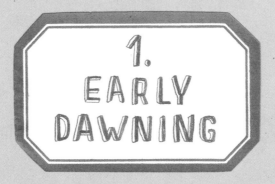

Our backyard in Karlsruhe,
in the south of Germany, faced a US military
air base, where planes regularly took off and landed.
I heard them hissing and roaring above our house
like dangerous animals that had — unbelievably —
decided to spare our lives.

Part of me understood that something
had once gone horribly wrong.

1980

me

my mother

You'll see ruins. You'll see flowers. You'll see some mighty pretty scenery. DON'T LET IT FOOL YOU. <u>You are in enemy country</u>.
You are up against German history.

<u>Chapter One</u>. The Führer? Bismarck. The title? "Blood and Iron." Nice country, Germany! Tender people, the Germans! <u>Chapter Two</u>. The new Führer: Kaiser Wilhelm. New title: "Deutschland Über Alles." And the same tender German people smacked us with their WWI!

We finally knocked that Führer out. We marched straight into Germany and said, "Why, these people are OK! It was just the Kaiser we had to get rid of! This is really some country! When it comes to culture, they lead the whole world!"

We pulled out our armies, and they flung <u>Chapter Three</u> in our faces. Führer number three: Hitler. Slogan number three:

"Today, Germany Is Ours. Tomorrow, the Whole World."

And Chapter Four? It can happen again. The next war.
The German lust for conquest is not dead. Practically every German
was part of the Nazi network. Practically everything you believe in,
they have been trained to hate and destroy.

The German people are not our friends. However sorry they
may seem, they cannot come back into the civilized fold just by
sticking out their hand and saying, "I am sorry."
Don't clasp that hand!
It's not the kind of a hand you can clasp in friendship.
Trust none of them.
Someday, the German people might be cured of their disease.
The SUPER-RACE DISEASE. The WORLD-CONQUEST DISEASE.

But they must prove that they have been cured
— beyond the shadow of a doubt —

before they ever again are allowed to
take their place among respectable nations.

Until that day, we stand guard.

That is your job in Germany.

My brother and I had never met any of the American soldiers who, since the end of the war, had been stationed in our town to protect us from resurging Nazism and the threat of Communism, but we knew quite a bit about them. Americans chewed gum; they put their feet on tables; they read DONALD DUCK in bed without taking off their shoes; and they still had the death penalty. They had given chocolate to our aunt Karin when she came back from evacuation in the countryside after the war — the first chocolate she had ever had.

The AMIS,
as we called them,
cruised the streets in their extravagant fake-wood-paneled cars and stopped in for hamburgers at the American supermarket, which we weren't allowed to enter because we didn't have American IDs. We used the word AMI-SCHICKSE for an American woman with pink fingernails and cotton-candy hair, not knowing that the term had originally been used in the 1940s for German women who fraternized with men from the American occupying force. We also didn't know that SCHICKSE was a Yiddish word. Nor, for that matter, what Yiddish was.

I don't remember when I first heard the word KONZENTRATIONSLAGER, but I became aware of it long before I learned about the Holocaust. I sensed that concentration camps were sinister places, and I imagined that the people who lived there were forced to concentrate to the point of physical anguish. But I was too afraid to ask, feeling that this was something embarrassing to talk about, something that grown-ups discussed in whispers, something evoking the same unsettling feeling as the man who sometimes gave candy and balloons to my brother and me when we were playing alone in the front yard.

**Are Jews evil?**

I asked my mother one day after coming home from elementary school. It was around the time that I had made it a habit to change into the panther costume she had sewn me for carnival.

**Of course they aren't!! Who told you that?**

She stopped stirring and vigorously rubbed her hands dry on her apron.

**My religion teacher said it was the Jews who killed Jesus.**

Not knowing any Jews, I assumed that they didn't exist outside of the Bible. They seemed distant, like a long-extinct species.

Experiencing my mother's anger, I concluded that day that Jews — all Jews — were good.

One of my favorite books as a child was DER STRUWWELPETER,
a collection of 19th-century illustrated stories about
children who get punished for misbehaving.

The book was considered outdated
because of its moral severity,
but my mother happened
to keep her old childhood
copy on the family bookshelf.

The story that
stuck with me most
was about a girl
alone at home with
her cats who plays with
matches and burns herself
into a heap of ash.

The girl's
demise was
depicted in
colorful
exaggeration.

What the story taught me was that you shouldn't
feel sorry for yourself if you were responsible
for your own downfall.

Throughout my childhood, the war
was present but unacknowledged,
like the heirloom lion's-head tureen
stored behind our usual dishware.

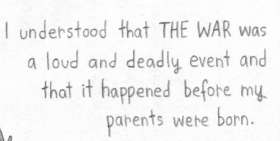

I understood that THE WAR was
a loud and deadly event and
that it happened before my
parents were born.

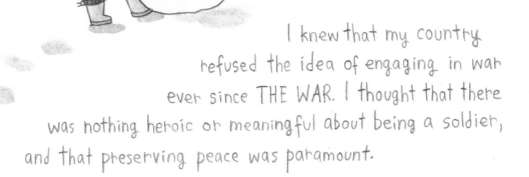

I knew that my country
refused the idea of engaging in war
ever since THE WAR. I thought that there
was nothing heroic or meaningful about being a soldier,
and that preserving peace was paramount.

The notion that other countries could
still be at war seemed to me like madness.

Though my parents weren't religious, they occasionally took my brother and me to church on Sundays when we were children, so that we would grow up believing in something. I remember waiting in line outside the confessional box, desperately trying to recall a guilt-evoking-enough incident to be confessed. Even though I didn't understand why JESUS DIED FOR OUR SINS, the concept of INHERITED SIN — as the Germans call ORIGINAL SIN — and of having to bear the consequences of another generation's actions seemed familiar, and I swore to Jesus that I would accept it.

After finishing my confession, I knelt down on the unforgiving wooden plank and made amends by saying four Hail Marys.

S. 41    Hausarbeit 9. 4. 91

Professor: Er steckt dadurch in einer Zwickmühle ⇒ Tod. (Angst
Schwester: Tod des Bruders. Anderes Ansehen im Getto. Angst.
Mitbewohner: Hass gegen die Deutschen. Trauer.
Leisten

r Post
silbert
nummer

I learned about the Holocaust in school around the
same time that my mother ceremoniously announced
to the family over dinner that I had had my first period.

She wanted to do me a favor by acting less
prudish than her own parents had, but for me,
the idea of being a woman seemed to be as
shameful as being a German.

A yellow Star
of David, which I
drew in my 9th-
grade exercise
book, to illustrate
a story on the
Holocaust.

Jude

One day my mother walked into my room
as I was sewing a yellow star with the word
JUDE onto the sleeve of my jacket.

"What are you doing?" she asked.
"I made this star and I'm going to wear it
out of solidarity with the Jews."
"I don't think that's a good idea."

I undid my work, confused.

Whenever I traveled abroad as a teenager, my guilt traveled with me.

"Just say you're from the Netherlands," my aunt Karin told me before each trip. I should have taken her advice.

I don't recall the first time I ever saw pictures of the Holocaust. I remember a film projector playing in a darkened, stuffy classroom. The images were of rubble and dust and dead bodies, accompanied by the sound of masculine voices. Was it NIGHT AND FOG that we watched in history class that day? Or was it just BEN-HUR?

After the war, the Allies forced civilians from the towns surrounding the camps to look at the dead bodies. "That was a very smart and important thing to do," my mother told me. Some of them were made to walk barefoot.

In some towns, the Allies forced local farmers to drive the bodies of the dead through the streets on the way to the burial site, for everyone to see.

We were taken on class trips to concentration camp museums in France, Germany, and Poland. I remember walking past the train tracks, the barracks, and the electric fences, past the poplar trees that looked too beautiful, documenting it all with my camera in black and white, trying to understand the scope of the atrocities committed — right here — by my own people: acts that cannot and should not ever be forgiven.

Two of the pictures I took were of my classmates. I labeled them in bold letters on the back:

"After our visit to the extermination site Birkenau, 1994."

I remember the sense of gratification I felt when I developed the photos in my basement and saw the images slowly emerge in their acid bath:

Here was the evidence of our collective guilt.

Excerpt from my 11th-grade exercise book: Analysis of an Adolf Hitler speech.
① Comment on Hitler's mode of reasoning and intention. ② Examine how Hitler uses linguistic devices.
③ Assess the effect that Hitler's speech had in the specific historic situation. ④ "Who possesses linguistic skills possesses people." Using examples, position yourself within the challenges of this statement.

Klassenarbeit Nr. 5                                            25.3.1994
Thema: Sprache des Nationalsozialismus        Text-/Zitaterörterung

Thema 1: Texterörterung

TAGESBEFEHL HITLERS AN DIE SOLDATEN DER OSTFRONT VOM 15.APRIL 1945
IN ERWARTUNG DER RUSSISCHEN GROSSOFFENSIVE AUF BERLIN

Zum letzten Mal ist der jüdisch-bolschewistische Todfeind mit seinen Massen zum Angriff angetreten. Er versucht, Deutschland zu zertrümmern und unser Volk auszurotten. Ihr Soldaten aus dem Osten wißt zu einem hohen Teil selbst, welches Schicksal vor allem den deutschen Frauen, Mädchen und Kindern droht. Während die alten Männer und Kinder ermordet werden, werden Frauen und Mädchen zu Kasernenhuren erniedrigt. Der Rest marschiert nach Sibirien.

Wir haben die Stunde vorausgesehen, und es ist seit dem Frühjahr alles getan worden, eine starke Front aufzubauen. Eine gewaltige Artillerie empfängt den Feind. Die Ausfälle unserer Infanterie sind durch zahllose neue Einheiten ergänzt. Alarm-Einheiten, Neuaufstellungen und Volkssturm verstärken unsere Front. Der Bolschewist wird dieses Mal das alte Schicksal Asiens erleben, d.h. er muß und wird vor der Hauptstadt des Deutschen Reiches verbluten.

Wer in diesem Augenblick seine Pflicht nicht erfüllt, handelt als Verräter an unserem Volk. Das Regiment... ... ihre Stellungen verlassen, benehmen sich so schimpflich, daß sie sich vor Frauen und Kindern, die in unseren Städten dem Bombenterror standhalten, werden schämen müssen.

Achtet vor allem auf die verräterischen wenigen Offiziere und Soldaten, die, um ihr erbärmliches Leben zu sichern, im russischen Solde, vielleicht sogar in deutschen Uniformen, gegen uns kämpfen werden. Wer euch den Befehl zum Rückzug gibt, ohne daß ihr ihn genau kennt, ist sofort festzunehmen und nötigenfalls augenblicklich umzulegen, ganz gleich welchen Rang er besitzt.

Wenn in diesen kommenden Tagen und Wochen jeder Soldat an der Ostfront seine Pflicht tut, wird der letzte Ansturm Asiens zerbrechen genau so, wie am Ende auch der Einbruch unserer Gegner im Westen trotz allem scheitern wird.

Berlin bleibt deutsch. Wien wird wieder deutsch, und Europa wird niemals russisch.

Bildet eine verschworene Gemeinschaft nicht des leeren Begriffs eines Vaterlandes, sondern zur Verteidigung eurer Heimat, eurer Frauen, eurer Kinder und damit unserer Zukunft.

Being FEHLERFREI (fault-free) was our universal goal. Our teachers' red pens divided our exercise books into right and wrong, and the red marks felt as reassuring in their clarity as they were unforgiving.

On the path from the Versailles Treaty to the Paris Peace Conference, my teenage classmates and I left no stone unturned. We analyzed Hitler's speeches alliteration by alliteration, tautology by tautology, neologism by neologism. We staged avant-garde theater performances on the anniversary of REICHSKRISTALLNACHT. We prepared questions for the old women who traveled from America to tell us about the camps, but we never thought to ask about one another's grandparents. We learned that our language was once poetic, but now potentially dangerous. We read Schiller but didn't learn to love him as we loved Shakespeare. We struck the German words for HERO, VICTORY, BATTLE, and PRIDE from our vocabularies. We avoided superlatives, and we used the word ZUSAMMENGEHÖRIGKEITS-GEFÜHL, the sense of identifying with a group and believing in an idea larger than oneself, when defining American cultural identity, but not our own.

We resorted to the expression "That's so typically German" to describe someone's unfriendly or narrow-minded behavior. We learned that VERGANGENHEITSBEWÄLTIGUNG means "coming to terms with one's political past," but felt that it really defined "the process of struggling to come to terms" with it. We learned that the German word for RACE should only be used to distinguish animal species, and ETHNIC only in the context of genocides; yet we felt that history was in our blood, and shame in our genes. But there were also gaps in our education: we didn't learn that tens of thousands of Germans had been killed for resisting the Nazi regime (because it would have made our grandparents who didn't resist look guiltier in comparison?), or that 150,000 men of Jewish descent had fought in the WEHRMACHT (because their participation would have made us feel less guilty?); we learned little about the losses endured during the Allied bombings, or about the millions of Germans who had been displaced from Germany's former eastern regions after 1945 (because we knew that feeling sorry for ourselves was wrong?). Because we never learned about contemporary Jewish culture, we associated the word JUDE strictly with the Holocaust and we understood that it could be uttered only in a whisper.

We never learned about **what** happened in our own hometown.

We never learned the lyrics to our national anthem.

We never learned old folk songs,

We struggled to understand the meaning of HEIMAT.

# Heimat
[ˈhaɪmaːt] *f (no plural)*
From the comprehensive German BROCKHAUS encyclopedia:

---

"That term which defines the concept of an imaginarily developed, or actual landscape or location, with which a person ... associates an immediate sense of familiarity. This experience is ... imparted across generations, through family and other institutions, or through political ideologies. In common usage, HEIMAT also refers to the place (also understood as a landscape) that a person is born into, where they experience early socialization that largely shapes identity, character, mentality, and worldviews ... The National Socialists used the term to ... associate a space of withdrawal, in particular for those groups that were looking to identify with a simplistic template for psychological orientation."

How do you Know who you are,

if you don't understand where you come from?

From the notebook of a homesick émigré

# Things German | Nº2 | *der Wald*

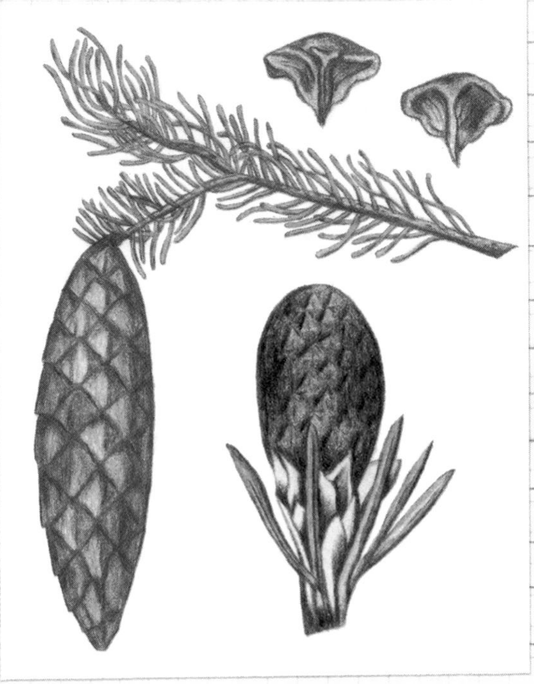

A woodpecker; an abandoned hunting stand; fingers of light; vertical silence. The forest makes me feel calm and protected unlike any other place. It is the "forests in their silence" that have kept old fairy tales alive, the Grimm Brothers once claimed. Their GERMAN DICTIONARY, begun in 1838, lists over a thousand nouns and adjectives containing the word WALD. My favorite ones are WALDEINSAMKEIT (forest-solitude), WALDFINSTERNIS (forest-obscurity), and WALDUMRAUSCHT (surrounded-by-a-rustling-forest). In 1852, the German Jewish author Berthold Auerbach stated that "French should be spoken at the salon, and German in the forest." During the 1936 Olympic Games, gold-medal winners were presented with a seedling of a German oak, a symbol for steadfastness. Several of these so-called HITLER OAKS still stand in the United States today. In 1938, the Reich's propaganda minister Joseph Goebbels considered barring Jews from "German forests." As part of the postwar reparations, the French and British military ordered the massive harvesting of German forests. In 1983, the term WALDSTERBEN (forest die-off) was included in the German thesaurus for the first time. A wave of existential angst washed over the country.

# 2.
# FORGOTTEN SONGS

Twelve years after my encounter with the old
woman on the rooftop of an apartment building,
I find myself on another New York City rooftop.

This time, I am not listening to a
Holocaust survivor's story, but to a singer's
live performance of Schubert's WINTERREISE.

And this time, with its longing for love and nature and
death, with its melancholy and its unembellished
beauty, my native language evokes longing,

rather than shame.

And yet, after all these years, I still try to hide my accent:

by covering my mouth while I speak,

Excuse me — do you know if there are any houses for sale in this area?

Yes, I think there is one on the next block.

by keeping my answers short,

Excuse me — are you Jewish?

No. (...)

by putting on

a different accent.

Hello. I'm Dr. Rosenfeld. What seems to be the problem?

I've had this kinda weird feeling in my left arm ... like, a floaty feeling, y'know?

Even though rabbis greet me with warmth and curiosity at the bar mitzvahs I attend, and even though some of my Jewish friends tell me that the Americans were as bad for killing the Indians and enslaving Africans, my shame hasn't disappeared. I can't even stretch and hold my right arm at an angle, like the other students in my yoga class, without thinking of the Hitler salute.

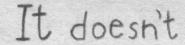

It doesn't

... I am told by strangers at parties that one should never travel to Germany (because it will always be the land of the Huns and the Nazis).

...the articles I read in the NEW YORK TIMES describe Germany as the "homeland of SCHADENFREUDE," a country defined by a "rule-driven culture" exhibiting traits such as "rigid adherence to principle and a know-it-all streak," where "VERBOTEN often becomes the first word to impress itself on the mind of a visitor."

help that...

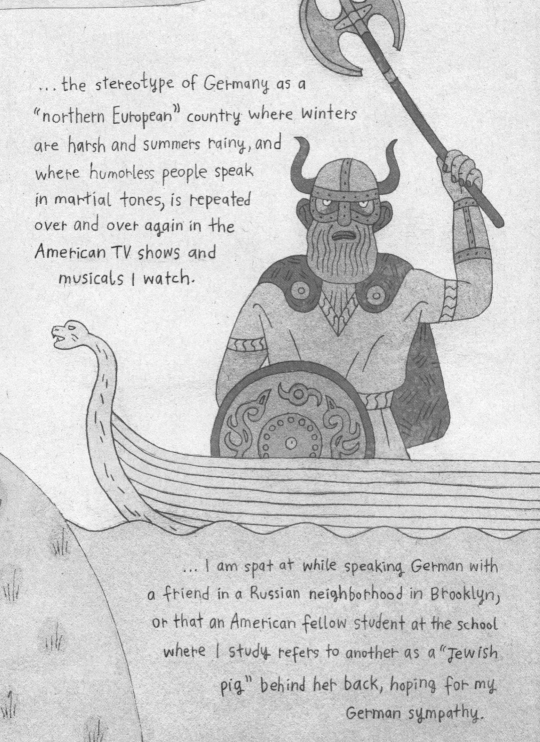

... the stereotype of Germany as a "northern European" country where winters are harsh and summers rainy, and where humorless people speak in martial tones, is repeated over and over again in the American TV shows and musicals I watch.

... I am spat at while speaking German with a friend in a Russian neighborhood in Brooklyn, or that an American fellow student at the school where I study refers to another as a "Jewish pig" behind her back, hoping for my German sympathy.

My husband grew up with a Christmas tree and a Jewish sense of humor. His mother came from a family of assimilated German Jews. When one of my mother's friends found out that he was Jewish, she was thrilled:

"A Jew from New York! They are the most intelligent people! I always wished I'd had a Jewish boyfriend so I could have made up for the horrible things our parents' generation did."

"I have only positive feelings about it," my mother told me when I asked how she felt about my marriage. "I just hope that his encounters with Germans are positive. The only other thing I am worried about is if you had a son and circumcised him. If history should ever repeat itself, I wouldn't want your child to be physically distinguishable from others."

For my father, becoming the father-in-law to a Jewish man meant "not quite making amends, but mending my relationship to Judaism."

Not

marrying a

has lessened my

Even though her family had always sworn never to support the land of the Nazis by buying a German car, my 80-year-old mother-in-law came to her grandparents' homeland for the wedding. The fact that I am German was never an issue for her.

"I don't care if you are German," her boyfriend told me, straight like the gin in his glass, the first day I met him on the patio of a cocktail bar in Florida, where he owns a condo. Yiddish was the only language he spoke growing up in 1920s Brooklyn.

"When I went to Israel for the first time and saw all the Mercedes on the streets, and people told me what the reparation payments had done for them, I stopped resenting the Germans. As long as you love this man, you're welcome, wherever you are from."

Now, my mother-in-law lives in an assisted-living facility, and she no longer remembers her trip to Germany. "Why on earth would I have gone there?" she asks in disbelief each time we remind her, and makes sure to jokingly advise us "not to trust them" when we return to Germany to visit my family.

even

Jewish man

German shame.

where absolution is given to those who confess their guilt on television shows; where biblical terms such as EVIL creep into presidential speeches, and where Adolf Hitler has evolved from a historic figure into the symbol of evil itself; where the bug sprays — FRONTLINE, COMBAT, RAID — are named with military terms; where diseases are BATTLED, rather than SUFFERED;

where people don't immediately think of the worst-case scenario, but believe that nothing bad will happen until it happens; and where being an adulterer can disqualify you from obtaining citizenship as easily as having been a member of the Nazi Party

— I feel more German than ever before.

The longer I've lived in my Caribbean
neighborhood in Brooklyn, the more I find
myself scavenging American thrift stores
for the green-stemmed Riesling glasses, the
vine-branch corkscrews, and the cuckoo clocks
I would never have thought to buy in Germany.

The longer I've been away, the more books
I pick up at the New York Public Library
about my hometown, to learn everything I can
about its wartime history. From this safe distance,
I allow myself to see the loss it once endured.

And yet, the longer I've lived
away from Germany, the more
elusive my idea of my identity
becomes. My HEIMAT is an echo,
a forgotten word once called
into the mountains.

An unrecognizable
reverberation.

# Field Notes, part 1: USA

In search of a HEIMAT untainted by the war,
I visit the STAMMTISCH (regulars' table), a group of
German and Austrian Jewish immigrants who have
been meeting in New York since 1943 to speak
German and maintain their sense of cultural identity.
The group's host recently turned 100.

They talk about the war and about starting
a new life in the "Fourth Reich," the neighborhood in Manhattan
where those who had
survived the Third
settled. They talk
about the lack of
universal healthcare
in America and about
the Democratic
presidential hopefuls.

I eat their homemade hazelnut cake and potato
salad, and I long to be loved by them

like a granddaughter.

"What does it mean to be German?" I ask 89-year-
old Trudy, sitting to my right. I am hoping for a
clear-cut answer, but all she says is "I don't know."

I practice German patriotism at the New York City Steuben Parade, an annual event named after a  prominent Prussian general, where proud Ameri- cans of German origin march alongside members of the LAS VEGAS MUSTACHE CLUB and the GERMAN DOG GROUP, the GERMAN HIKING CLUB, and the SWABIAN SINGING CLUB of New Jersey.

I'm given the first German flag I've ever touched, but because I cannot bring myself to wave it, I discreetly slip it into my bag, only to be given another, then another, and another. I march uneasily, hoping that no one in the cheering, cowbell-ringing crowds that line the sidewalk will recognize me. I ask a 40-something German tourist on the sidewalk why she came to the parade. "It's about time that Germans feel confident about their country again," she says, and waves her little paper flag.

Have I been away from Germany so long that I have missed a crucial turning point?

I travel to Milwaukee, where Germans settled during the 1800s, long before the guilt set in, where the streets smell of hops, and where national pride is displayed even by the dogs who run the annual German Dachshund Derby Race in dirndls.

I scavenge local junk stores for old photo plates and other evidence of 19th-century midwestern German life and eat

liver-dumpling soup at a 100-year-old restaurant on Old World Street. I attend an Oktoberfest celebration at a nursing home, where elderly women hum along as an a cappella group sings about lost love and peaceful forests in German. I fight a bout of sentimentality while watching people — women wearing dirndls and men sporting lederhosen and Republican Party pins — swirl around to the rhythm of the polka at a German dance festival. Most people here are descendants of the Danube-Swabians —ethnic Germans who were displaced from Eastern Europe after WWII.

VAL.BLATZ
BREWING COMPANY
1845     1895

"Being German is my life," the organizer of the festival, a woman my age wearing edelweiss-shaped earrings, tells me. "We are the lifers. We live it. We breathe it." Her German pride makes me uncomfortable, but it also makes me envious. As I watch the dancing

girls with braided blond hair, I find myself feeling sad over not being able to feel it, too, angry about not being able to identify with my culture, or any ethnic heritage, the way it seems to come so naturally to Americans.

I feel like a traitor to these Americans with whom I am supposed to share my German pride, a spy from a country that exists entirely inside myself, that has no banner and no anthem, a nation with only one inhabitant. Nobody suspects that I'm a spy; my glass is topped up with Riesling and I am stuffed with bratwurst and given a ride back to my hotel, and my name is added to a mailing list.

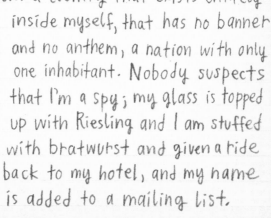

# Back home,

I find an email from the woman with the edelweiss-shaped earrings in my in-box:

"The pain suffered by the Jewish people during WWII is well known. The pain suffered and the death toll of the Eastern German people is not known at all. An expulsion turned genocide has been a well-kept secret for over 60 years. By clicking on the link below and signing the electronic petition, you are asking PBS to broadcast the documentary MILLIONS CRIED... NO ONE LISTENED."

I delete it.

My search has yielded no satisfactory answers. I decide to look where it seemed impossible to look before.

# Field Notes, part 2: Germany

I return to Germany during the World Cup in 2014, where, on TV, politicians and university professors discuss the appropriateness of displaying the German flag. In Berlin, the streets are filled with soccer fans who don't sing along when the national anthem is played before kickoff; cars display stickers saying DEUTSCHLAND— NEIN DANKE (Germany—no thank you); members of the anti-fascist movement call for the elimination of everything that bears the colors of the German flag and shout, "Wer Deutschland liebt, den können wir nur hassen" (whoever loves Germany deserves nothing but hate); a woman with a T-shirt saying HEIMAT— WOANDERS IS AUCH SCHEISSE (HEIMAT — everywhere else is shitty, too) passes by me in the street; and a drunk man asks for my prediction as to who will win the game. When I ignore him, he condemns my behavior as "typically German."

"We shouldn't get too elated now," the German coach warns on TV, after the German team scores seven goals against Brazil. More than 95,000 Nazi references are posted on Twitter on the day of the game. The next day, the NEW YORK TIMES writes:

"Brazil Left Humiliated by Germany's Dominance" and "the Germans were merciless" and "a soccer massacre of the highest order."

I seek refuge from the postgame tumult in grubby thrift shops
and look for clues to the HEIMAT I can only halfheartedly embrace.

I see steep rocks to be conquered

and rapid rivers to be crossed.

I see deep, fern-filled forests to be hiked with furry leather backpacks and walking sticks;

forests to be searched for mushrooms and hunted for the antlers of bellowing stags;

forests inhabited by witches and wolves, veined with paths abandoned by red-caped little girls, marked with bread crumbs to show the way home;

forests to write poems and sing songs about.

I see yellow fields of rapeseed and hear the song of the skylark.

I see hills neatly combed into grapevines and remember a forgotten song.

I see snow-covered fir trees and the traces of deer sniffing out chestnuts.

I see deep valleys with torrential rivers where bare-

breasted sirens drown sailors with their beautiful voices.

And as I look, I feel
as though someone were
watching me from behind.

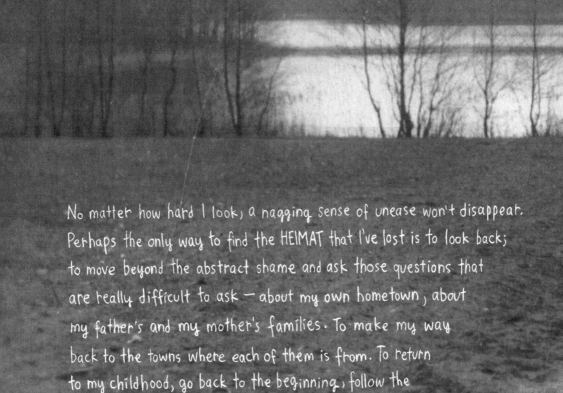

No matter how hard I look, a nagging sense of unease won't disappear. Perhaps the only way to find the HEIMAT that I've lost is to look back; to move beyond the abstract shame and ask those questions that are really difficult to ask — about my own hometown, about my father's and my mother's families. To make my way back to the towns where each of them is from. To return to my childhood, go back to the beginning, follow the bread crumbs, and hope they'll lead the way home.

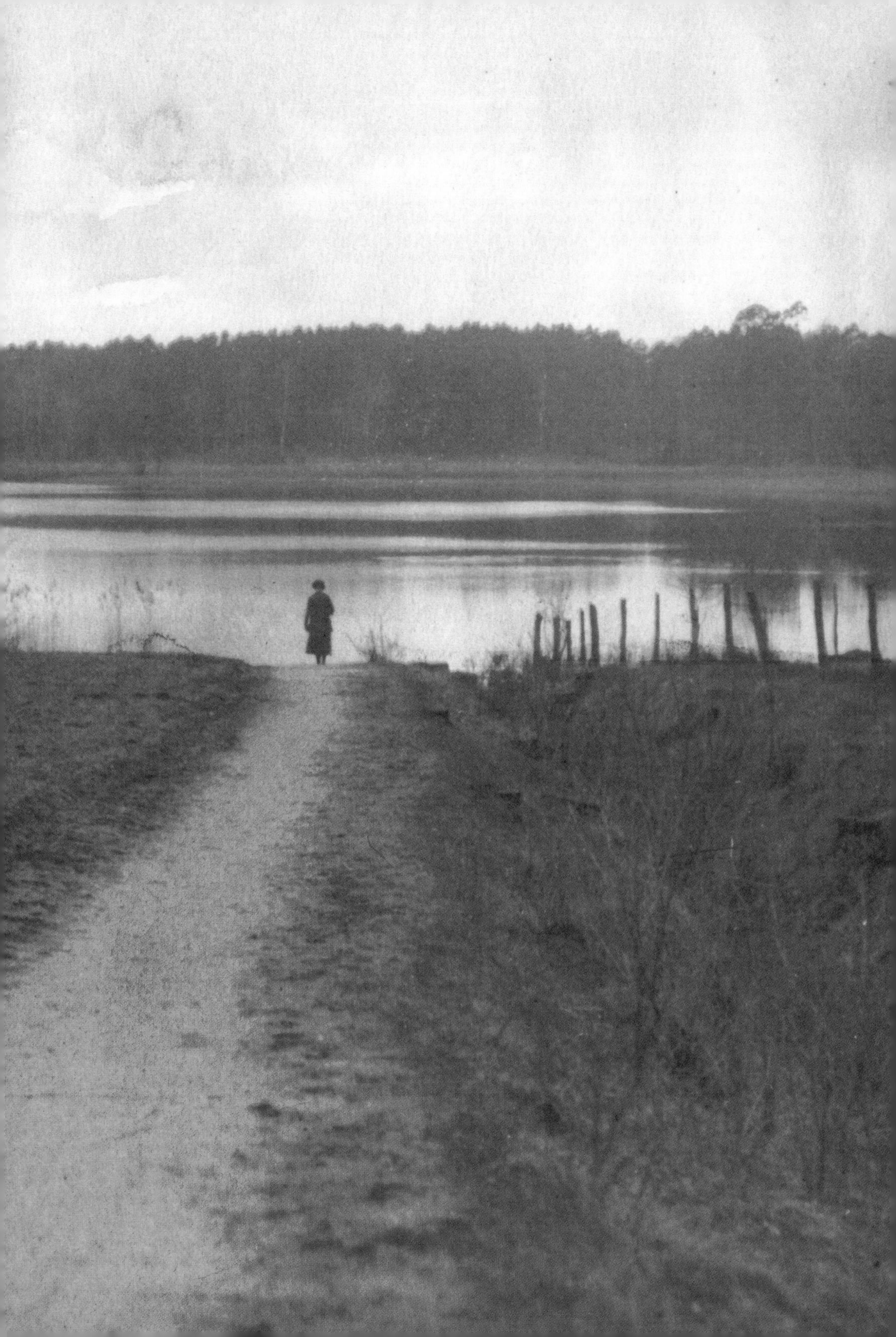

# 3.
# POISONOUS MUSHROOMS

Every year, we went to Italy for a family vacation.

To us, Italy represented everything Germany didn't have, or, perhaps, elements it once had, but lost, in the perfectionist reconstruction of the postwar years. Here, we could feel uninhibited and live the exotic fantasy of southern-European life. We spent days driving around in our non-air-conditioned green Volvo,

exploring small medieval towns, sampling local delicacies, visiting remote museums,

and following in the footsteps of famous artists, writers, and filmmakers.

On one of those excursions, we came upon a large military cemetery.

The cemetery's geometric precision was intimidating. Near the entrance, we found an inscription in German.

# SELIG SIND, DIE DA LEID TRAGEN, DENN SIE SOLLEN GETRÖSTET WERDEN.

BLESSED ARE THEY WHO ARE SUFFERING, FOR THEY SHALL BE COMFORTED.

Buried beneath our feet lay the bodies of not Italian but German WWII soldiers. A few decades after the end of the war, 30,683 of them had been dug up from nearby provisional graves for identification and finally reburied here.

The cemetery was vast. We made our way through the labyrinth in silence.

Suddenly, my father disappeared.

Papa

Wait!

What are you looking for?

My brother.

After a while we spotted him in the distance. He walked briskly and held a piece of paper in his hand.

I'd always known that I had an uncle who died young, at age 18.

"He fell in the war," my father used to say, but nobody in my family seemed to know how or where he was killed. I knew that my uncle had been the heir to my grandparents' land in Külsheim, a tiny town in southwest Germany surrounded by fields, forests, and vineyards. I knew that my father was born a few years after my uncle's death, and that his parents had named him Franz-Karl, after his dead brother.

I knew that because my uncle had died, they expected my father to inherit and tend to their farm, to look after the animals, the fields, and the plum trees.

And I knew that my father had never fulfilled that expectation.

My father, ca. 1947.

As a child, I discovered a musty-smelling box in the drawer of the mahogany cabinet in our living room. It contained old photographs of my uncle and a few of his 6th-grade school exercise books.

Their stories described the life cycle of the maybug and the history of European forestry, the heroic Viking adventures and the havoc of the 30 Years' War, the importance of charity and the necessity for personal hygiene, the Führer's difficult childhood and his reintroduction of Mother's Day to celebrate German women and their Aryan children.

besser für einen Zeichner geeignet. 5. Dort muß er Speis tragen. 6. Er fragte: „Keiner." 7. oder sie warfen ihn hinunter.

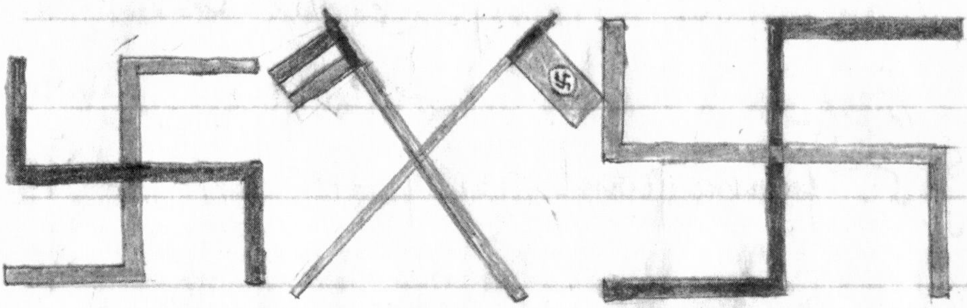

Nr. 2.

Wie ich mein Mütterlein ehrte.

Als ich am Muttertag aufgewacht bin, bin ich schnell aus dem Bett und hab mich angekleidet. Dann bin ich schnell in den Garten und habe einen

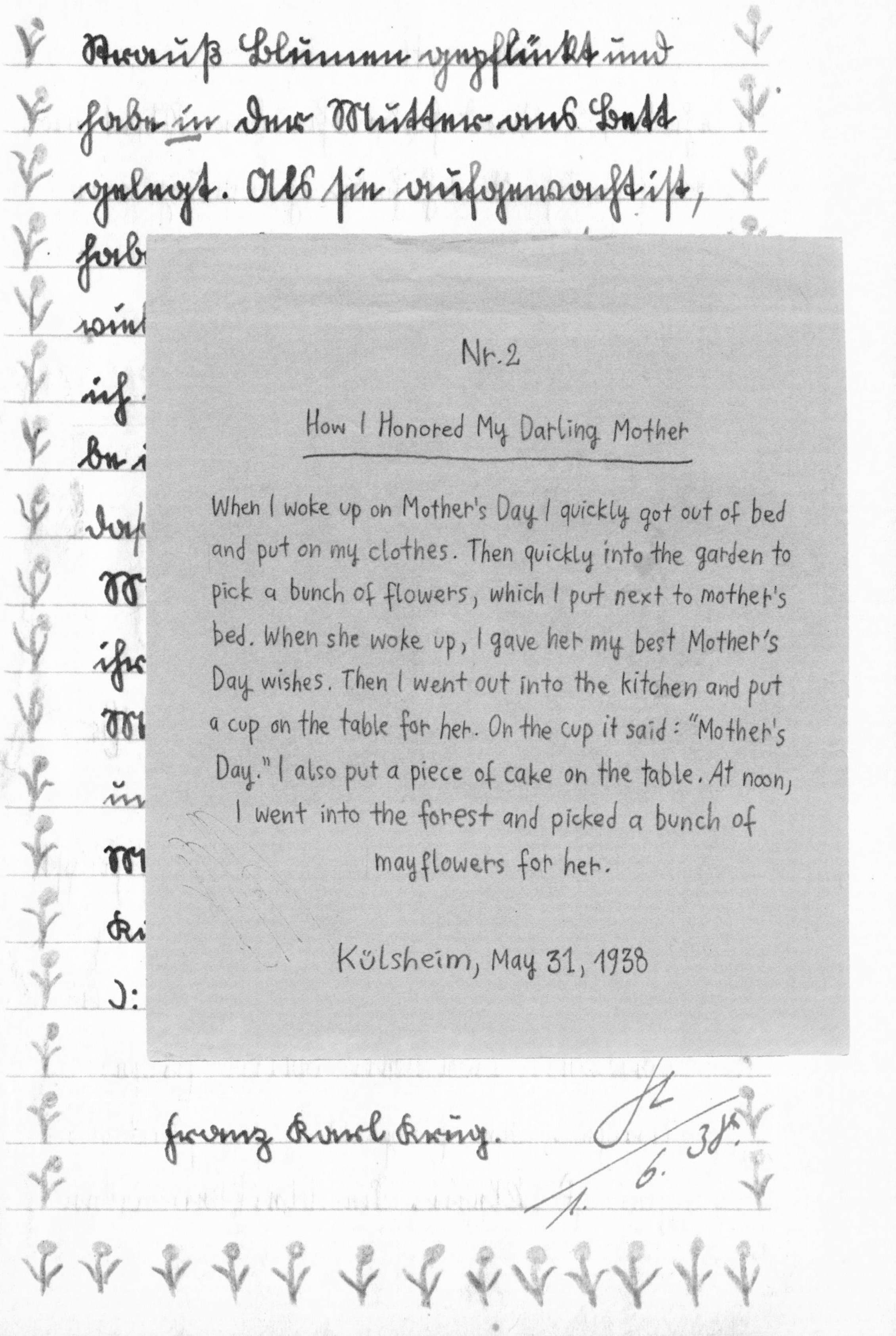

Strauß Blumen gepflückt und habe ihn der Mutter ans Bett gelegt. Als sie aufgewacht ist,

Nr. 2

How I Honored My Darling Mother

When I woke up on Mother's Day I quickly got out of bed and put on my clothes. Then quickly into the garden to pick a bunch of flowers, which I put next to mother's bed. When she woke up, I gave her my best Mother's Day wishes. Then I went out into the kitchen and put a cup on the table for her. On the cup it said: "Mother's Day." I also put a piece of cake on the table. At noon, I went into the forest and picked a bunch of mayflowers for her.

Külsheim, May 31, 1938

Franz Karl Krug.

1. 6. 38.

All throughout my father's childhood,
his mother told him that his brother had been
a sweet and well-behaved boy,

unlike my father, who was a stubborn and
ill-tempered child. My father skipped days of
kindergarten, then skipped school, playing all by himself
on the grounds of Külsheim's medieval castle.

My uncle was a complete stranger to me.
I didn't know anyone who had known him.

War and death were the only things I associated with him.
Because he had been one of Hitler's soldiers, I learned early on
that I wasn't supposed to feel sadness over his premature death.

His photos and exercise books were the only physical evidence
of his existence, and I tried desperately to find him somewhere
in between the lines of his propagandistic essays.
It was like searching a concrete wall for cracks and leaks.

Examining the stories written in my uncle's neat handwriting, and the illustrations with which he carefully decorated the margins, was an intimate but chilling experience. The books intrigued me, but I never showed them to any of my friends.

Mein Kampf
Nr. 8.
Die ewige Wache.
Am 9. November 1923 fielen sechzehn deutsche Männer vor der Feldherrnhalle in M

lich die Freiheit. 2. die Rüdinger forderten
uns ... und ... 3.
... ... ... Entscheidungsspruch.
4. Im 12. Jahrhundert herrschte in
Bremen ein Erzbischof Gerhard II.
5. Erklärter. 6. Rüdingeren. 7. ... Jahr...

2.000

... sich
... Herrs-

Nr. 11

The Jew, a Poisonous Mushroom

When you go to the forest and you see mushrooms
that look beautiful, you think that they are good.
But when you eat them, they are poisonous and can kill
a whole family. The Jew is just like this mushroom.

When you see the Jew from afar, you don't immediately
recognize him. But if you talk to him, you recognize
him immediately. He pretends to be nice and flatters
you shamelessly. Just like the poisonous mushroom can
kill a whole family, the Jew can kill a whole people.

Külsheim, January 20, 1939

## Nr. 11.

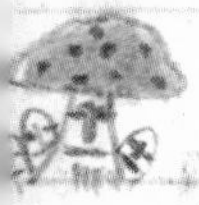
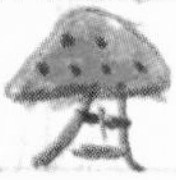

### Der Jude, ein Giftpilz.

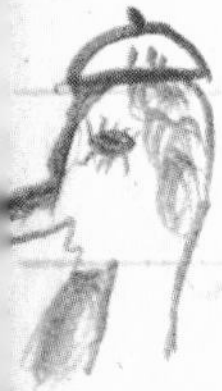

Wenn man in den Wald geht und man findet Pilze, die schön aussehen, meint man, diese wären gut. Aber wenn man sie ißt, sind sie giftig und können eine ganze Familie töten. So wie dieser Pilz ist, ist auch der Jude. Wenn man den Juden von weitem sieht, erkennt man ihn sofort nicht, aber redet man mit ihm, so erkennt man ihn gleich. Er tut schön und schmeichelt einem ins Gesicht. So wie der Giftpilz eine Familie töten kann, so kann

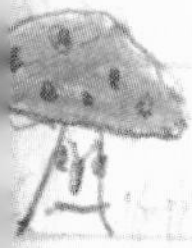
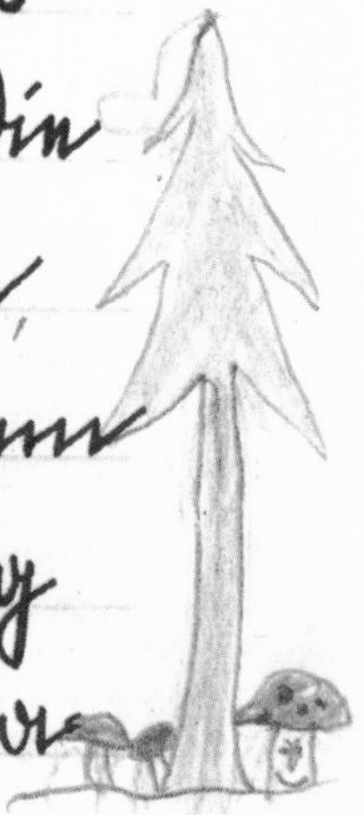
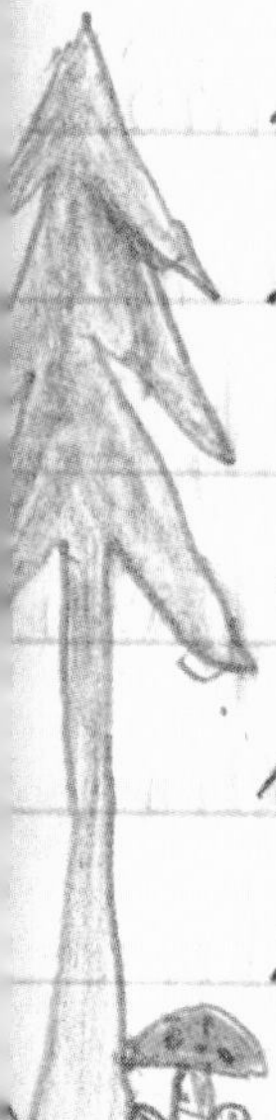
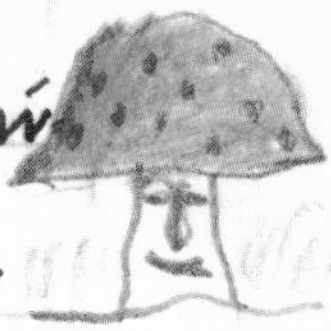
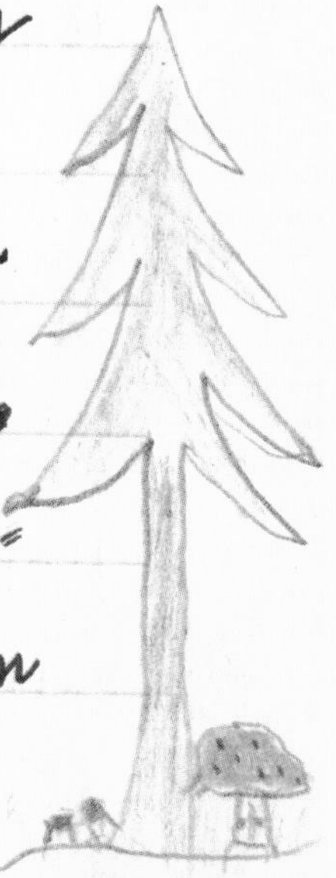
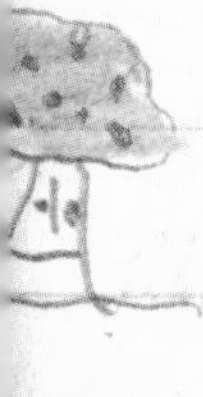

From the notebook of a homesick émigré

# Things German | №3 | das Pilze-sammeln

Collecting mushrooms with my family; examining each mushroom carefully and comparing it to the corresponding picture in the PILZ-FÜHRER (mushroom guidebook) before placing it in the woven basket; back home, scrubbing off the bits of earth on the stem and in between the gills, and then sautéing the mushrooms in a pan with butter, salt, and pepper and eating them with a piece of dark rye bread. By eating the mushrooms I feel as if I've become part of the forest. The poisonous red, white-polka-dotted mushroom is depicted in many German children's books. On New Year's Day, it is a symbol of good luck that appears on greeting cards and in marzipan sweets made in its shape.

My mother, dressed as a poisonous mushroom, 1953.

(Costume made by my grandmother.)

To this day, she remembers the moment the picture
was taken because of how disappointed she was that
she couldn't be a princess, instead.

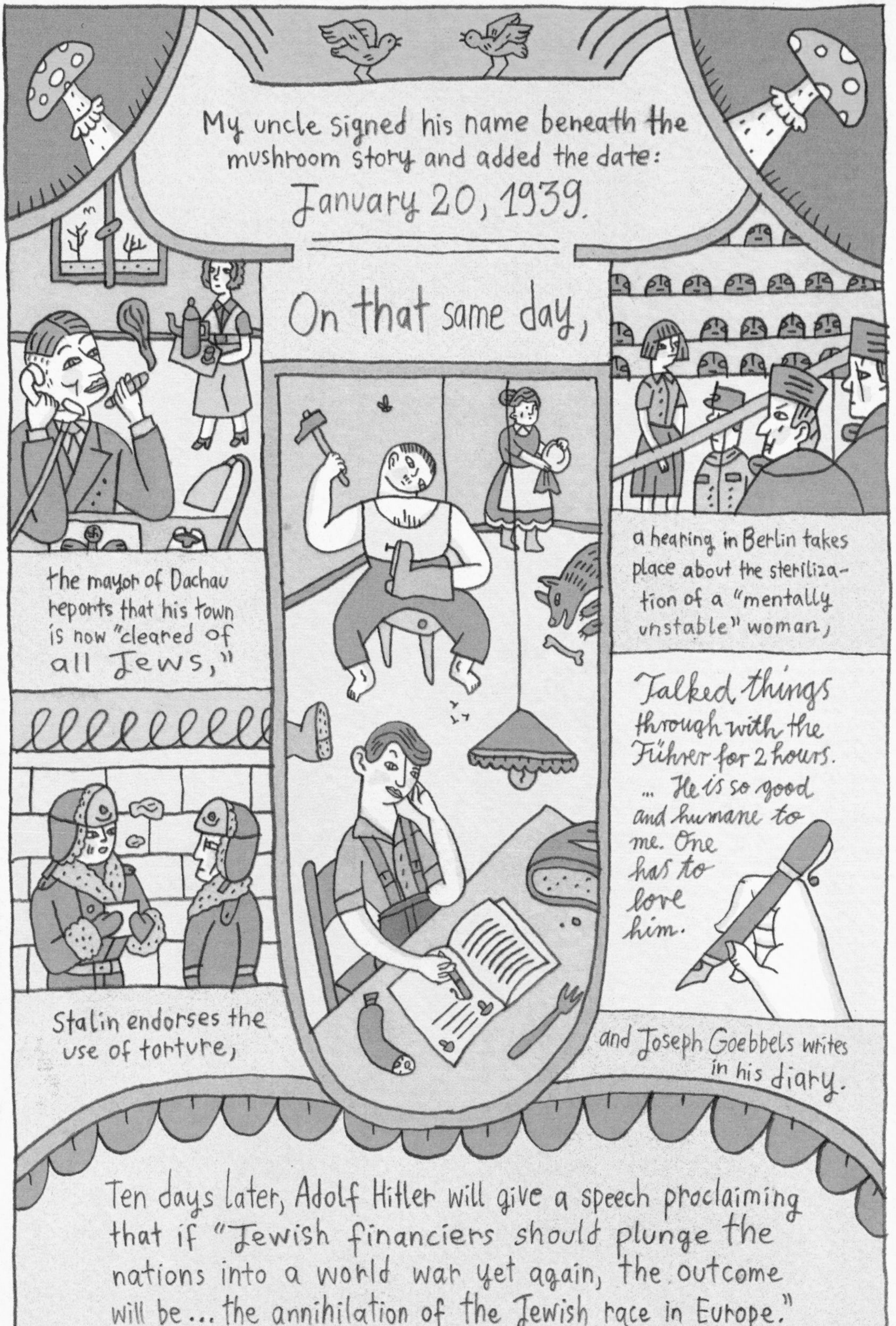
My uncle signed his name beneath the mushroom story and added the date:
January 20, 1939.
On that same day,
the mayor of Dachau reports that his town is now "cleared of all Jews,"
a hearing in Berlin takes place about the sterilization of a "mentally unstable" woman,
Stalin endorses the use of torture,
Talked things through with the Führer for 2 hours. ... He is so good and humane to me. One has to love him.
and Joseph Goebbels writes in his diary.
Ten days later, Adolf Hitler will give a speech proclaiming that if "Jewish financiers should plunge the nations into a world war yet again, the outcome will be ... the annihilation of the Jewish race in Europe."

Was my uncle's story influenced by THE POISONOUS MUSHROOM, the 1938 collection of anti-Semitic children's stories?

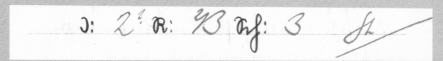

The teacher marked three spelling mistakes and two grammatical mistakes in the mushroom story, gave it a B for its content, and signed it "St."

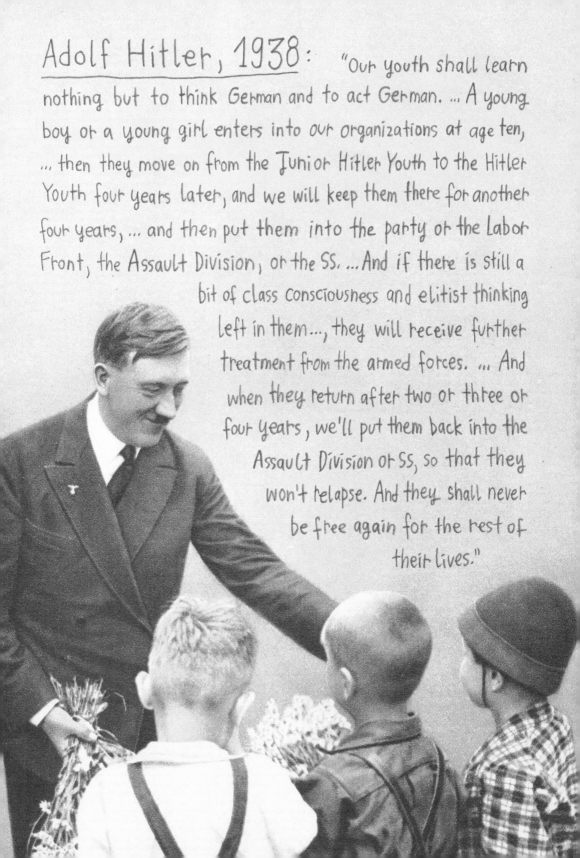

**Adolf Hitler, 1938:** "Our youth shall learn nothing but to think German and to act German. ... A young boy or a young girl enters into our organizations at age ten, ... then they move on from the Junior Hitler Youth to the Hitler Youth four years later, and we will keep them there for another four years, ... and then put them into the party or the Labor Front, the Assault Division, or the SS. ...And if there is still a bit of class consciousness and elitist thinking left in them..., they will receive further treatment from the armed forces. ... And when they return after two or three or four years, we'll put them back into the Assault Division or SS, so that they won't relapse. And they shall never be free again for the rest of their lives."

My uncle was born in 1926. In 1936, the National Socialists announced that 90% of all children born in 1926 had successfully been recruited into the Hitler Youth. By 1939, joining had become mandatory.

Külsheim is a small town. Jews and Christians lived side by side, engaged in trade for centuries. My uncle probably knew the Jewish boys and girls who lived in town. He was twelve years old when he wrote the story in his exercise book. Too young to understand the power of Nazi propaganda. But old enough to understand that Jews are not like poisonous mushrooms.

b. toy made in honor of Führer's birthday: €4

a. caricature of Jew: €.20

c. Hitler Youth trading cards: set of 10, €2

d. brooches given in exchange for Winter Relief donations: €4 each

e. primer: €1

**Schneeballschlacht!**

"Der Schnee backt fein", ruft Heinz. "Kommt, wir bauen eine Burg und machen eine Schneeballschlacht." "O ja!" "Das ist fein!" "Alle ran!" Bald stehen die Wände der Burg. An den Ecken werden noch zwei Türme aufgesetzt. Nun kann die Schlacht losgehen.

Schon wird die Mannschaft in zwei Haufen. "Ihr greift an!" Jeder macht sich nun die Schnee-

"Brr", macht Otto und schüttelt sich, er ist an den Hals getroffen. Werner wälzt sich lachend im Schnee, er ist über seine eigenen Beine gestolpert. "Du bist totgeschossen", necken ihn die andern.

Dreimal müssen die Angreifer stürmen, erst beim vierten Male sind sie Sieger. Der linke Turm steht noch, da stecken sie ihre Hakenkreuz-fahne drauf.

"Noch einmal", ruft Otto, "aber jetzt wollen wir die Angreifer sein!"

**Der Schneemann.**

Seht den Mann, o große Not!
Wie er mit dem Stocke droht,
gestern schon und heute noch!
Aber niemals schlägt er doch.
Schneemann, bist ein armer Wicht,
hast den Stock und wehrst dich nicht.

82

15

When I finally caught up with my father at the cemetery, it turned out that he had walked up to its chapel and, for reasons unknown even to himself, had scanned the names in the register. There, among the thousands of names his eyes rested on for a fraction of a second —

names that had once been called from kitchen windows at dinnertime; names written on Christmas gifts and school exercise books; names spoken severely in classrooms; names pronounced ceremoniously by mayors on enlistment day; names whispered by girls and women the night before departure;

names shouted out on the battlefield when a response could no longer be expected; names reported to superiors; names spelled out on clacking typewriters in colonels' secretaries' offices; names read, reread, and read again on damp military stationery; names chiseled into stones; names remembered quietly by mothers and fathers before a final breath was taken —

— among all these unfamiliar names belonging to people unknown to him, my father found what he had been looking for:

HIS OWN NAME.

The number on the piece of paper my father was holding specified the exact location of my uncle's grave. The gravestone was meticulously maintained.

FRANZ-KARL KRU

OBERGRENADIER

4.6.1926 – 16.7.19

Inscribed on it was the name that my uncle and my father had always shared.

For the first time, I experienced the loss of my uncle's life in a physical way. Briefly, he emerged from the depths of the heavy mahogany cabinet, not as a shadow, but as a human being whose eyes I could have looked into and said, "Uncle," who could have given me a goat as a gift for First Communion, whose children's outgrown clothes I could have worn, and to whom I could have sent a post-card from Italy that summer, telling him about our visit to a German WWII cemetery that was filled with gravestones inscribed with the names of total strangers.

Standing at his grave, I longed to understand what it had felt like to be him. Was he proud to fight in the war? Was he afraid? What was the last thing he saw, the last thought he had?

"This is the closest I've ever been to my brother," my father said.

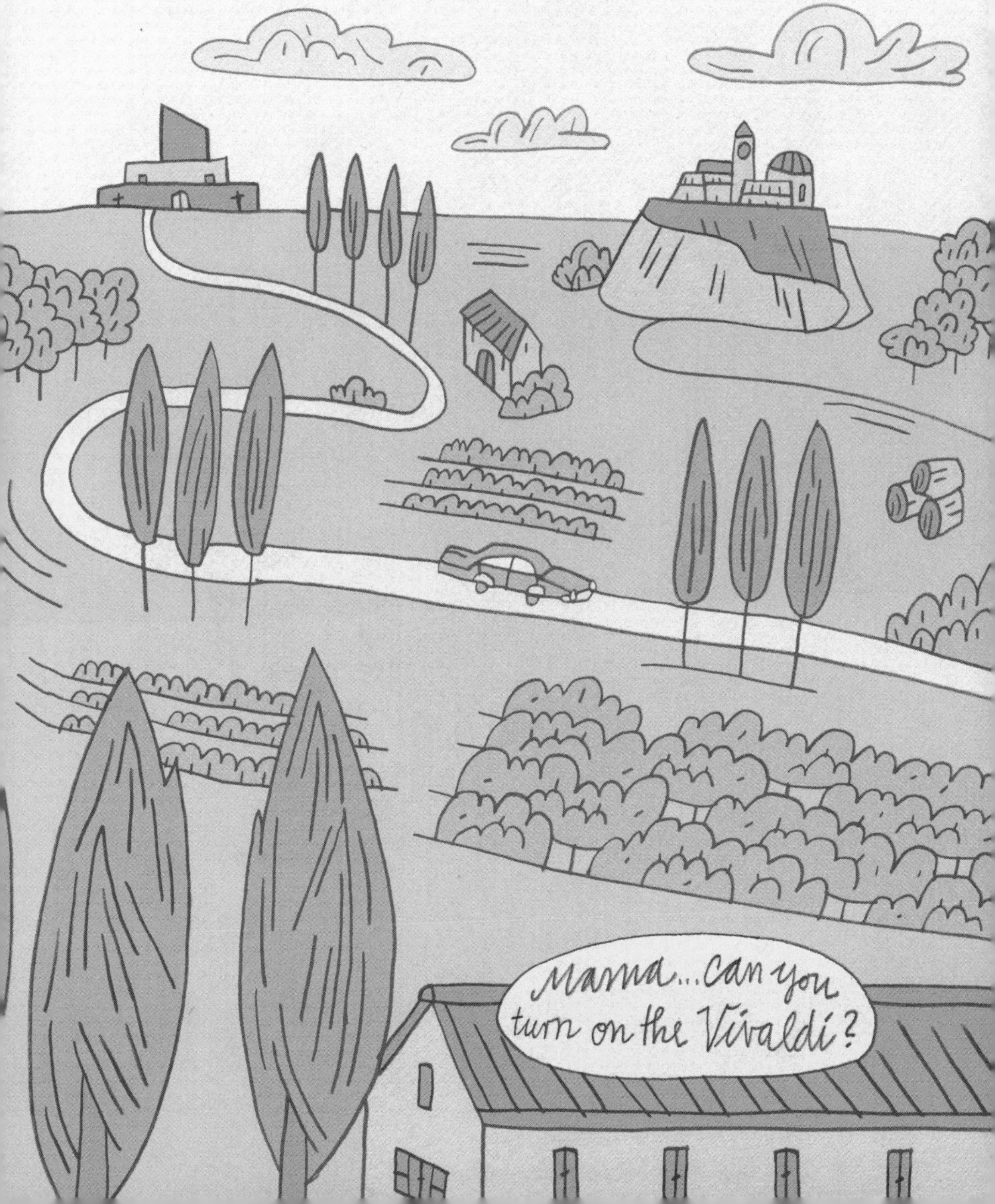
Mama...can you turn on the Vivaldi?

Two photographs, placed     on top of each other, match perfectly.

Two arms, each
holding a First
Communion candle.

Two arms, each
holding a hymnbook.

The new face
that emerges
looks directly
at me.

# 4.
# KEEPING
# TIME

My mother grew up in the age of oblivion.

She was born in 1946 in Karlsruhe, my hometown. All that played on German television in the 1950s were escapist romance dramas set in Alpine and Black Forest landscapes.

When she was sixteen, she discovered a left-wing magazine about the Holocaust in a garbage can. She had already learned about Germany's atrocities at school, but the photographs in the magazine were the first ones she had ever seen of the camps. Terrified, she confronted her father.

"What did he say?" I asked her when I was a teenager myself.

"I don't think my father was a Nazi. He told me he didn't like Hitler because of the way he screamed all the time. I remember once overhearing a conversation my parents had with friends over coffee. 'Nobody knew what was happening to the Jews,' they said. 'But six million sounds a bit exaggerated.'"

My grandparents, Willi and Anna, ca. 1952.

"Grandpa wanted me to give this to you on your sixteenth birthday," she said. "I think he got it in the army." The watch's crystal was broken, but it still kept perfect time. I snapped it onto my belt loop, carried it with me everywhere, and wound it up incessantly. I pressed it against my ear and imagined Willi lying somewhere in a muddy trench, listening to the same relentless metallic ticking.

It was the image I associated with men of his generation.

I remember only a few moments with my grandfather:

when, one Christmas, he gave me the battery-operated barking dog that my mother would never have bought me; when, to my horror as a child, he killed a harmless spider by stamping on it in the garage of my parents' house; and when he choked on a potato croquette at the fancy restaurant with the pink tablecloths where we went on special occasions.

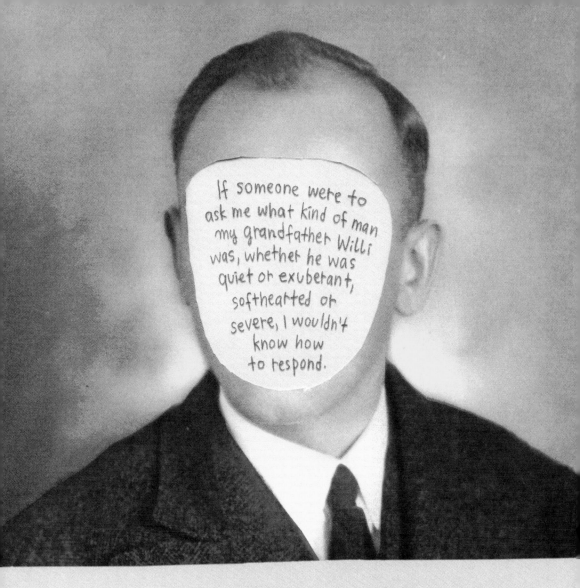

If someone were to ask me what kind of man my grandfather Willi was, whether he was quiet or exuberant, softhearted or severe, I wouldn't know how to respond.

Willi and Anna never showed me photographs or told me stories of their lives. They never talked about their youth. It didn't occur to me that at one time they were young until I learned about the war in school. My mother didn't talk about them much, and when she did, it was with the kind of weariness one feels when having to revisit a subject thought or talked about too many times before. In my mind, a family began with one's parents and ended with oneself.

Willi's wife, Anna, died of a heart attack in 1982. Her body was laid out at the mortuary behind a glass wall and surrounded with bouquets. Six years later, Willi died, too. My mother stood in her apron in the kitchen with red-rimmed eyes. He was 86. I was 11. Both of my father's parents had died before I was born. There were no grandparents left in my life.

The photographs I had never been shown migrated into the old shoebox in the bottom drawer of our living-room cabinet, along with my uncle Franz-Karl's exercise books.

When I close my eyes, I can remember every detail of my grandparents' apartment. The hallway with the mothball-scented flannel hat that rests on the coatrack; the Black Forest clock with the cuckoo that my grandfather silenced by gluing shut its window to the world; the living-room cabinet with Bambi, the china deer that returned my gaze with equal shyness through the glass; the clinking of flowered coffee cups on flowered saucers resting on flowered tablecloths; the severity of my grandfather's oak desk with its Leitz ring binders and the spongy green-and-orange stamp moistener that was always wet.

# Things German |  | *der Leitz-Aktenordner*

The binder, named after its inventor, Louis Leitz, was developed in 1896, in an attempt to establish order during Germany's increasing bureaucratization. Its sturdiness promises durability, its utilitarian design accountability. In New York City, the Leitz binder is the German consulate's binder of choice, and it is imported together with its matching hole punch. The Leitz binder has provided reassurance in matters of utmost importance in my life: health insurance, life insurance, birth and death certificates. ORDNUNG MUSS SEIN (order is essential) and ORDNUNG IST DAS HALBE LEBEN (order is half your life's battle) are German sayings. ALLES IN ORDNUNG (everything is in order) means that you have nothing in the world to worry about.

Over the years, by asking my mother and Aunt Karin, I pieced together the story of Willi's life.

Willi was born in Karlsruhe in 1902. He had a younger brother, Edwin, and a younger sister, Frieda, who died early.

For Willi's confirmation, his father, a factory worker, could only afford to buy him a suit made of paper. The suit was black, and when it rained on Confirmation Day, Willi turned as gray as the sky.

Put your hands on the table!

Eat up!

Willi's mother died when he was 16.

His father had her portrait mounted on a pair of cuff links and soon remarried.

Two years later, Willi's father died of an internal obstruction, and his widow decided that her home no longer had room for the stepchildren.

Willi was 18 and, from that moment on, took care of his 11-year-old brother. Wherever they went, Willi and Edwin linked their pinkies in order not to lose each other.

Carl Benz, the man who first patented the motorcar, came from Karlsruhe, and car mechanics were in high demand there. To support himself and his little brother, Willi trained in a garage...

... and sent Edwin to work as a VERDINGKIND, a child laborer in the countryside.

On the weekends, Willi went to visit Edwin.

This should be an easy fix!

One day, Willi met Anna, the daughter of a milkman. They married in 1930.

Willi found himself a position as a chauffeur with a Jewish linen salesman. He loaded the trunk with sacks of bedsheets, hand towels, and tablecloths and drove his employer to the countryside to sell the linens as dowry to people looking to marry off their daughters.

What did they talk about on their long rides through the country?

Did they become friends over the years?

"They had a very good relationship," my aunt Karin used to tell me.

"At some point, the employer told him that he had to 'go away.'

Willi

He gave Willi a large sum of money, to thank him for their good work relationship."

Was the story my grandfather told her about the Jewish linen salesman really true?

Or was it just a postwar family fantasy, like the one about Willi's having hidden his Jewish employer in the shed in his mother-in-law's backyard? Or like the one about Willi's supposed Jewish roots, "because of the way he looked," and because his mother, the woman on the cuff links, had had red hair?

Even though nobody had ever found, or even looked for, the slightest evidence of Jewish ancestry in our family, the conjecture promised comfort to my guilt-ridden teenage mind. As a young woman traveling abroad, I would mention the possibility with ill-founded confidence when asked where I was from.

Willi accepted his employer's money and bought himself a car. Soon after, he started his own driving school.

When the war began, he was recruited as a driving teacher for soldiers at the "home front" and was thus spared from duty at the front line.

The Jewish employer had perhaps saved my grandfather's life with his generous gift. But by doing so, he had also indirectly supported the German war effort.

My mother's and aunt's sense of relief when they told me the story reassured me. The image of Willi lying in the muddy trench was replaced with a new one:

that of him sitting motionlessly, eternally glued to the gray leather seat in his car, while other men commit atrocities far, far away.

Willi's brother, Edwin, completed an apprenticeship as a stonecutter and took to the road in search of work.

He made it all the way to Switzerland and into the arms of a woman named Elsa.

While Elsa looked after their two children, Edwin built church steps and, in his free time, played soccer and performed as a juggler.

In the spring of 1943, only a couple of months before becoming a Swiss citizen, Edwin received a letter from Germany.

German stonecutters weren't needed in Switzerland. They were needed at the front line.

What language is that?

This is the BBC.

SHH!

Edwin was ordered back to Germany, taught how to fire a gun, and sent to Russia.

Elsa and the children remained in neutral Switzerland.

After one year, Edwin returned to Germany on furlough. Elsa grabbed the children, stuffed their teddy bears with coffee beans for Anna to sell at the black market, and boarded a train to Germany.

The journey was interrupted by an Allied air raid.

Hours later, they arrived at Willi's house.

*Heil Hitler!*

*Home on furlough, Mr. Rock?*

*Drei Liter!*

When greeted in the street, Edwin responded with a phrase that sounded like the Hitler salute, but only meant THREE LITERS.

*The children are German, like me. If I desert, they'll be stateless!*

When Willi heard the stories from the front line, he suggested that his little brother desert. But Edwin rejected the idea.

ACHTUNG ACHTUNG!

QUICK!!

In anticipation of Allied bomb attacks, the children were put to bed in their street clothes. Then, one night, the alarm was raised.

*Look, Mama! Christmas trees!*

*We are almost at the bunker.*

Karin was mesmerized by the British parachute flares, used to illuminate the target area. They were the most beautiful things she had ever seen.

a. Pilot's snapshot: €2

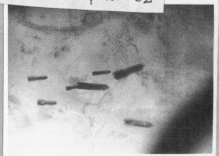

b. Child's drawing: €.50

c. Program for mock evening's entertainment during Allied bombing, singed on left during 1943 bomb attack.
Activities include:
Cheerful Overture, performed by the Municipal Siren Orchestra; opening remarks by the bunker warden; outdoor fireworks. €1

d. Membership ID for German Lifesavers' Union: €.25

DEUTSCHE LEBENS-RETTUNGS-GESELLSCHAFT E.V. · BERLIN

GRUNDSCHEIN

2. Februar 1944.

e. Letter from C. to his sister, M.: €.50

Liebe Martha!

Nichts höre ich ...
gesund bist oder ...
Du mußt in de...
voller Angst ausgestanden haben. Sei so gut,
gib mir sofort Nachricht, damit ich beruhigt
bin. Von Else weiß ich nicht einmal die
Adresse!! Von der Hanna habe ich auch keine

"I've had no news from you. I don't know if you're well, and if you're still alive! You must have suffered nights full of anguish in that old cellar. Please get in touch immediately so that I can get some peace of mind."

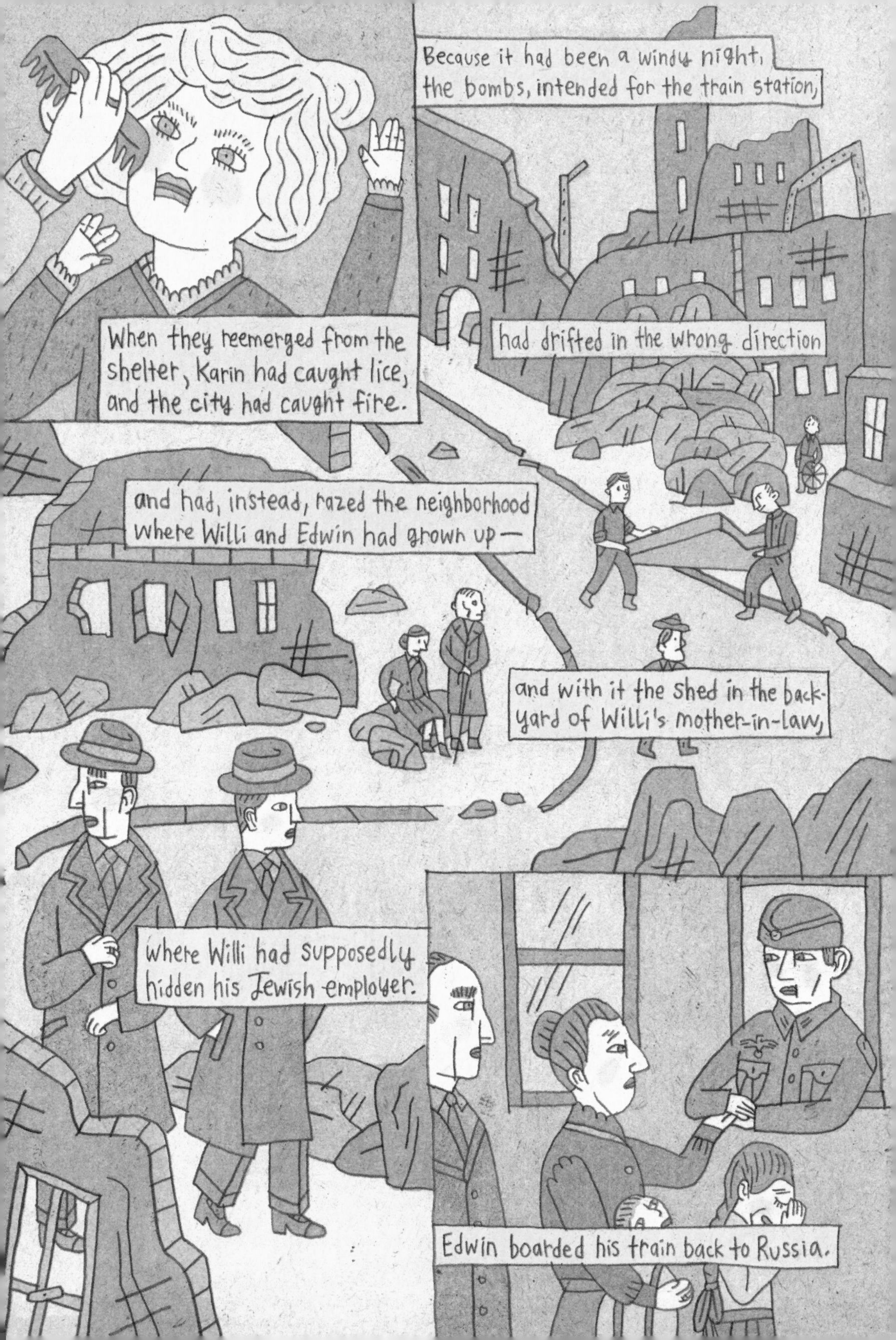
When they reemerged from the shelter, Karin had caught lice, and the city had caught fire.
Because it had been a windy night, the bombs, intended for the train station,
had drifted in the wrong direction
and had, instead, razed the neighborhood where Willi and Edwin had grown up—
and with it the shed in the back-yard of Willi's mother-in-law,
where Willi had supposedly hidden his Jewish employer.
Edwin boarded his train back to Russia.

5.
UNHEALED
WOUNDS

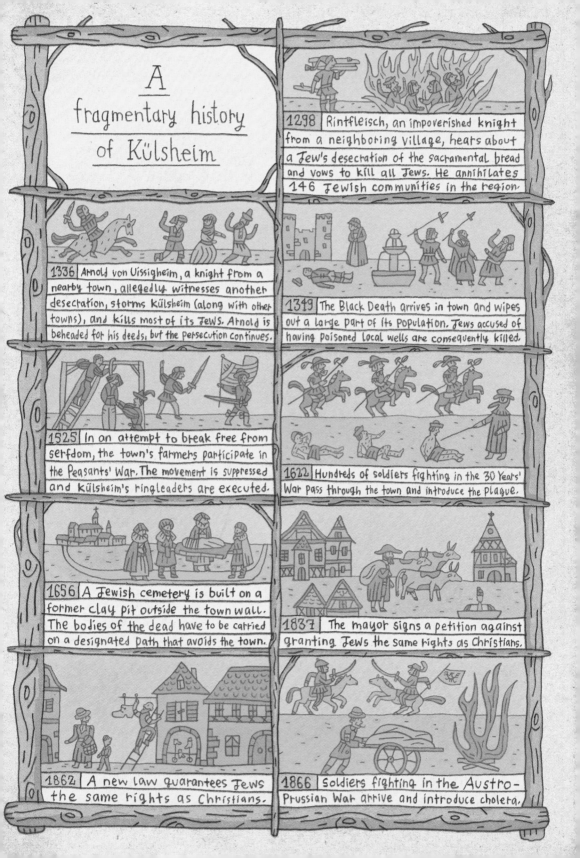

# A fragmentary history of Külsheim

**1298** Rintfleisch, an impoverished knight from a neighboring village, hears about a Jew's desecration of the sacramental bread and vows to kill all Jews. He annihilates 146 Jewish communities in the region.

**1336** Arnold von Uissigheim, a knight from a nearby town, allegedly witnesses another desecration, storms Külsheim (along with other towns), and kills most of its Jews. Arnold is beheaded for his deeds, but the persecution continues.

**1349** The Black Death arrives in town and wipes out a large part of its population. Jews accused of having poisoned local wells are consequently killed.

**1525** In an attempt to break free from serfdom, the town's farmers participate in the Peasants' War. The movement is suppressed and Külsheim's ringleaders are executed.

**1622** Hundreds of soldiers fighting in the 30 Years' War pass through the town and introduce the plague.

**1656** A Jewish cemetery is built on a former clay pit outside the town wall. The bodies of the dead have to be carried on a designated path that avoids the town.

**1837** The mayor signs a petition against granting Jews the same rights as Christians.

**1862** A new law guarantees Jews the same rights as Christians.

**1866** Soldiers fighting in the Austro-Prussian War arrive and introduce cholera.

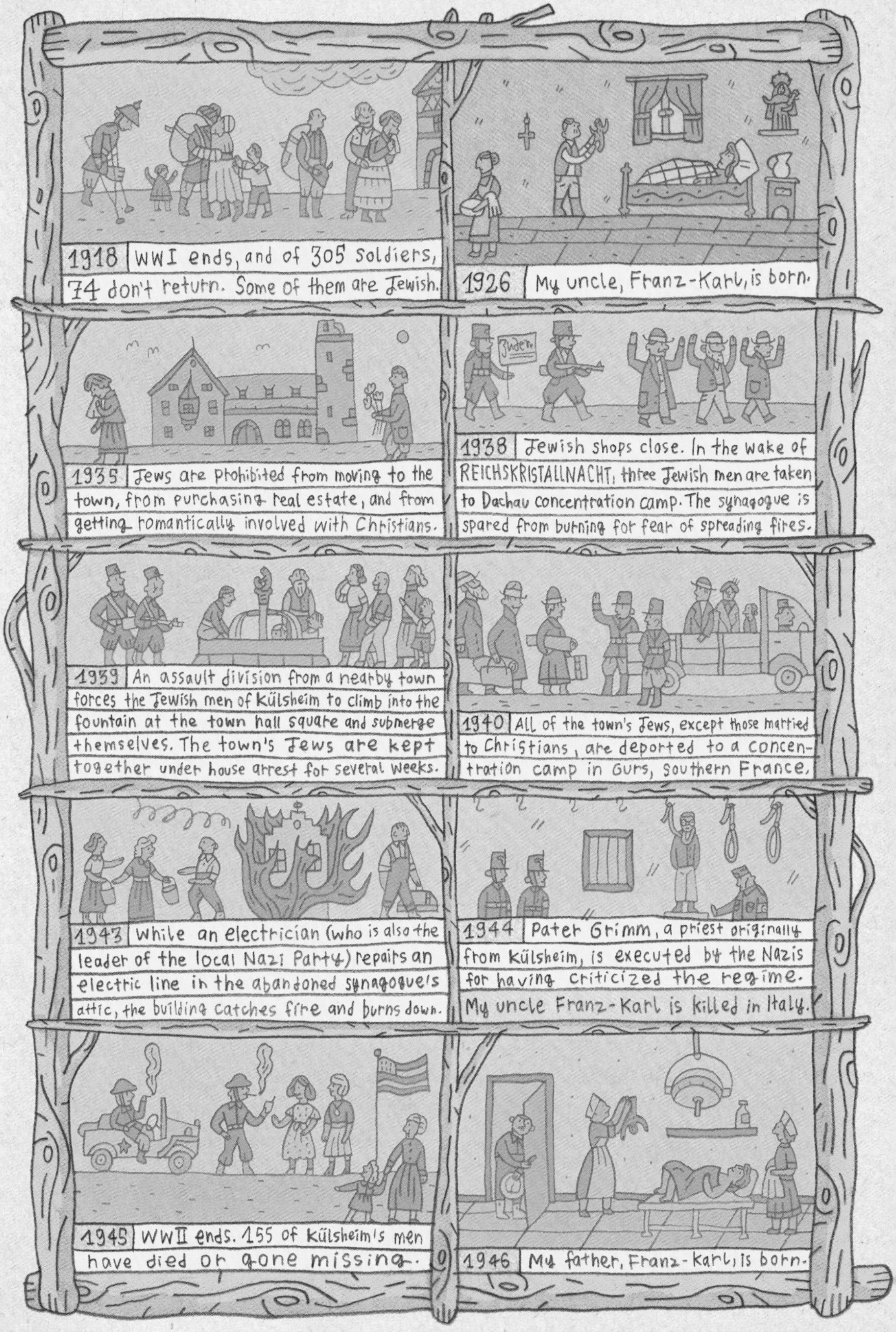
1918 WWI ends, and of 305 soldiers, 74 don't return. Some of them are Jewish.
1926 My uncle, Franz-Karl, is born.
1935 Jews are prohibited from moving to the town, from purchasing real estate, and from getting romantically involved with Christians.
Juden
1938 Jewish shops close. In the wake of REICHSKRISTALLNACHT, three Jewish men are taken to Dachau concentration camp. The synagogue is spared from burning for fear of spreading fires.
1939 An assault division from a nearby town forces the Jewish men of Külsheim to climb into the fountain at the town hall square and submerge themselves. The town's Jews are kept together under house arrest for several weeks.
1940 All of the town's Jews, except those married to Christians, are deported to a concentration camp in Gurs, Southern France.
1943 While an electrician (who is also the leader of the local Nazi Party) repairs an electric line in the abandoned synagogue's attic, the building catches fire and burns down.
1944 Pater Grimm, a priest originally from Külsheim, is executed by the Nazis for having criticized the regime. My uncle Franz-Karl is killed in Italy.
1945 WWII ends. 155 of Külsheim's men have died or gone missing.
1946 My father, Franz-Karl, is born.

My father was born on August 6ᵗʰ, 1946,
the day Germany returned Hungary's looted gold reserves.

He was an infant in 1947 when his father, Alois, died as a result of
falling off a tractor. Alois left behind his farm and fields; a hunting
rifle; a WWII shotgun; his blank KRIEGSTAGEBUCH, a diary given to
soldiers as a gift by the Führer; and a handful of photographs.

Despite the mustache—which fell out of fashion soon after the war ended—Alois little resembles a fervent Hitler supporter in his photographs.

Rather, he looks like an actor playing a Nazi in a foreign WWII comedy, his small, stout body unintentionally ridiculing the self-important gallantry of the soldiers surrounding him.

Alois was one of the first men in town to own a car. Because he was one of Külsheim's wealthiest farmers,

everyone referred to him as "The Lord."

My father never knew much about his father, or his grandparents, or, in fact, anyone else in his family. No shared family narrative was delivered from father to son to grandson, told over and over through generations.

And because there was no story, there also was no history.

"A farm woman's wild weed" is how my father describes his childhood self.

Growing up without a father, he was free to skip school, play tricks on the people in town, or sell crates of beer taken from his maternal grandfather, Heinrich (who owned the Rose—a local restaurant with greasy cast-iron pans and chairs with spread legs like those of a cow about to give birth—and who occasionally invited my father over for a bowl of bone-marrow-dumpling soup), to the American soldiers at the military camp for much more than they were worth. He giggles mischievously when he tells me these stories, and for a short moment he manages to bridge the abyss that lies between him and his difficult childhood.

I'll go as far as getting a paternity test!

To my grandmother Maria, being a mother meant often letting my father go to school without breakfast because she liked to sleep in, and sending him to bed alone, to his room in the attic that he shared with a few sacks of flour and a family of mice.

It meant letting rumors be spread about herself and the man who lived in the shed behind her house (because his house in Cologne had been bombed), and who dyed WWII uniforms black so that they could be worn as regular clothes.

It meant inadvertently teaching my father about the risks of trusting others when she acted as a guarantor for yet another man she fell in love with, who disappeared when his venture failed, forcing her to sell everything her husband had left her, to settle her lover's debts.

It meant abandoning my father to the priests at the Catholic boarding school where he lived from age eleven to twenty, and where students could choose between the stick or the belt.

I wish you'd die already!

It meant joining the Jehovah's Witnesses and therefore making my father the only child not allowed to return home for the summer, because the priests thought that she, a member of a controversial religious sect, couldn't be trusted.

It meant merely standing by and watching while her brother, Uncle August, a butcher, who later fell to his death from a beam in his barn, vented his anger at my father.

Külsheim for my father was nothing but an open wound.

After graduating from monastery school, he left to study in Karlsruhe. All that he took with him from Külsheim were his mother's demijohn of plum schnapps from the basement and his father's two rifles from under the floorboards, where Alois had hidden them when the Americans arrived. When Maria died, he returned to the old farmhouse, took some of his brother's photographs and exercise books, and left

— only returning in his dreams.

My father talks about his childhood as if it had been lived by someone entirely unrelated to him. "Let's change the subject," he says whenever I ask him about it. What he means is that no questions be asked about Annemarie — the aunt whom I have never met, his sister, who is fourteen years his senior and to whom he hasn't spoken since the year before I was born.

# 6.
# LOOKING
# INSIDE

Because my mother hardly ever talked about her parents, the only times when I was growing up that I looked at their old photographs was when my mother asked me to get fresh candles from the drawer that held the shoebox in the living-room cabinet. Sometimes, I would take a handful of photographs and ask her to explain them to me.

Often, she would respond by

frowning at the sight of my grandparents' apartment, of the flowered tablecloths, the severe oak sideboards, and the paintings of tranquil German landscapes and romantic Spanish street scenes — at the 1950s and '60s middle-class stuffiness she tried to escape by reading Russian novels and watching French films, and dreaming of traveling to Italy one day.

Now, about twenty-five years later, when I return to Karlsruhe, I decide to open the drawer again. Here is the same soapy smell of the candles, the same old shoebox with its worn corners, the same pictures, still in disarray. I remove the box from the drawer and bring it back to Brooklyn.

Only a handful of Willi's photographs point to his wartime experience.

Written on the back of one is
3/5/44 ATTACK ON KARLSRUHE.

Another shows a group of
soldiers digging a road.

The rest feature my grandfather in military uniform with my grandmother Anna and my aunt Karin. Except for the national eagle insignia,
his Wehrmacht belt, and the number 5 embroidered on his shoulder board,
Willi's uniform looks unadorned.

Images of men in Wehrmacht uniforms, some historical, some contemporary,
pop up on my screen as I look online for clues about Willi's uniform.
I sit stiffly in my chair at the café in Brooklyn, trying to use my torso as a
shield to hide the swastikas and SS insignia from the people sitting behind me.
I make my grandparents' faces disappear on some of the photographs and
post them on a forum dedicated to the "discussion on the axis nations."

"No Holocaust denial is tolerated," the website states, but some of the comments make me wonder about its political integrity.

In the "For Sale & Wanted" category, someone from Scotland is looking for uniform accessories in preparation for his first reenactment meeting.

A woman from the United States offers her grandfather's SS belt buckle for $400, but is told, "NOBODY pays TOP DOLLAR for something this ordinary."

Someone in Hong Kong sells miniature Russian houses with lift-off roofs so that figures can be placed inside to fire guns from the windows.

A couple in the Czech Republic replicates WWII German military and soccer shoes that feature swastika insignia on the soles. They are the most skillfully crafted shoes I've ever seen.

With its 199,742 visitors, the "Men's Hairstyles"
category is the forum's most viewed thread.

"I am widely interested in the hairstyle
of German men during the Third Reich,"
D.R. from Sweden posts.
"If anyone has good pictures, I'd
very much appreciate seeing them."

"I myself have a German haircut,"
D. replies from Germany, and posts
pictures of his head from various angles.
None of them show his face.

"Damn nice haircut.
Looks very Aryan! 😃"
applauds M.E. from Kuala Lumpur.

"Cool hairdo," asserts O. from Montreal.
"Want to print and take to barber tomorrow."

"As uncomfortable as it may be,"
K.D.F. chimes in, "you should ask for an
Adolf Hitler style."

I. in the Czech Republic writes,

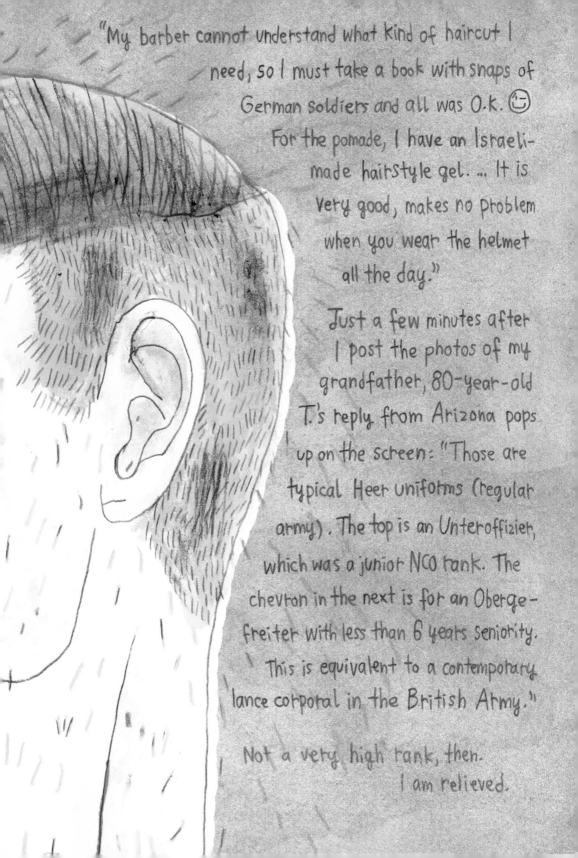

"My barber cannot understand what kind of haircut I need, so I must take a book with snaps of German soldiers and all was O.k. 😊 For the pomade, I have an Israeli-made hairstyle gel. ... It is very good, makes no problem when you wear the helmet all the day."

Just a few minutes after I post the photos of my grandfather, 80-year-old T.'s reply from Arizona pops up on the screen: "Those are typical Heer uniforms (regular army). The top is an Unteroffizier, which was a junior NCO rank. The chevron in the next is for an Obergefreiter with less than 6 years seniority. This is equivalent to a contemporary lance corporal in the British Army."

Not a very high rank, then. I am relieved.

When I was a teenager,
my aunt Karin told me
that after the Germans
invaded Belgium, Willi
was stationed in West
Flanders, in a seaside
town called Knokke. I
had always assumed
that he spent the entire
war at the "home front."

Finding out about his proximity to the Western Front worried me.
In between the photographs in the shoebox I find an old souvenir
booklet with pictures of Knokke: water, sand, parasols; people
strolling along the boardwalk; boys in bathing suits on the shore,
carrying sticks, looking for shells. Snapshots of peace and perfect happiness.

Toward the end of the war,
Karin said, Willi was taken
as a prisoner of war. I felt
reassured. Not only had he
worked for a Jewish man
who liked him. Not only
was he possibly half or a
quarter Jewish himself.
The fact that he had been
punished for having been a German soldier was particularly comforting.

# Things German | Nº5 | die Wärmflasche

The hot water bottle provides comfort when you are cold, sick, or troubled. A common evening ritual at home was for my mother to ask everyone in the family before bedtime, "Do you want a hot water bottle?" She kept at least three of them in the house. One German manufacturer sells 3.6 million bottles

annually worldwide, although sales remain low in America. My husband considers them messy and old-fashioned. One of the most popular German designs for hot-water-bottle fabric covers features a leaping stag. German hot water bottles are made of 100% recyclable material and comply with international medical standards. Some models come with a two-year "watertightness guarantee." Their reliability, durability, and safety are as reassuring as the heat they radiate.

Now, twenty years later, as I look at the images of Flanders again, I discover another booklet in the shoebox that I had overlooked: SOLDBUCH, ZUGLEICH PERSONALAUSWEIS (pay book, also identity card).

I carefully dissect its contents.

According to the SOLDBUCH, Willi was equipped as a soldier, but not a heavy fighter; he was declared unfit for field service on November 20, 1942, and, instead, ordered to serve as a driver; he returned on furlough in October 1944 because his office had been bombed; he was treated for a chest and pelvic-joint injury at a field hospital near Karlsruhe on April 1, 1945; his passport was destroyed in an Allied bomb attack on April 28, 1945; he lived in the American sector on July 18, 1945, where he was officially released from military service; and he was clearing rubble in Karlsruhe in 1946.

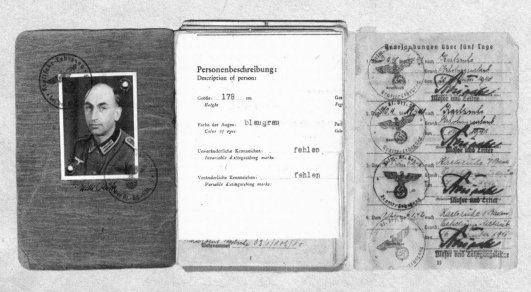

Knokke was liberated by the Canadian army on November 3, 1944. If the dates in the SOLDBUCH can be trusted, it is unlikely that Willi ever was a prisoner of war in Belgium.

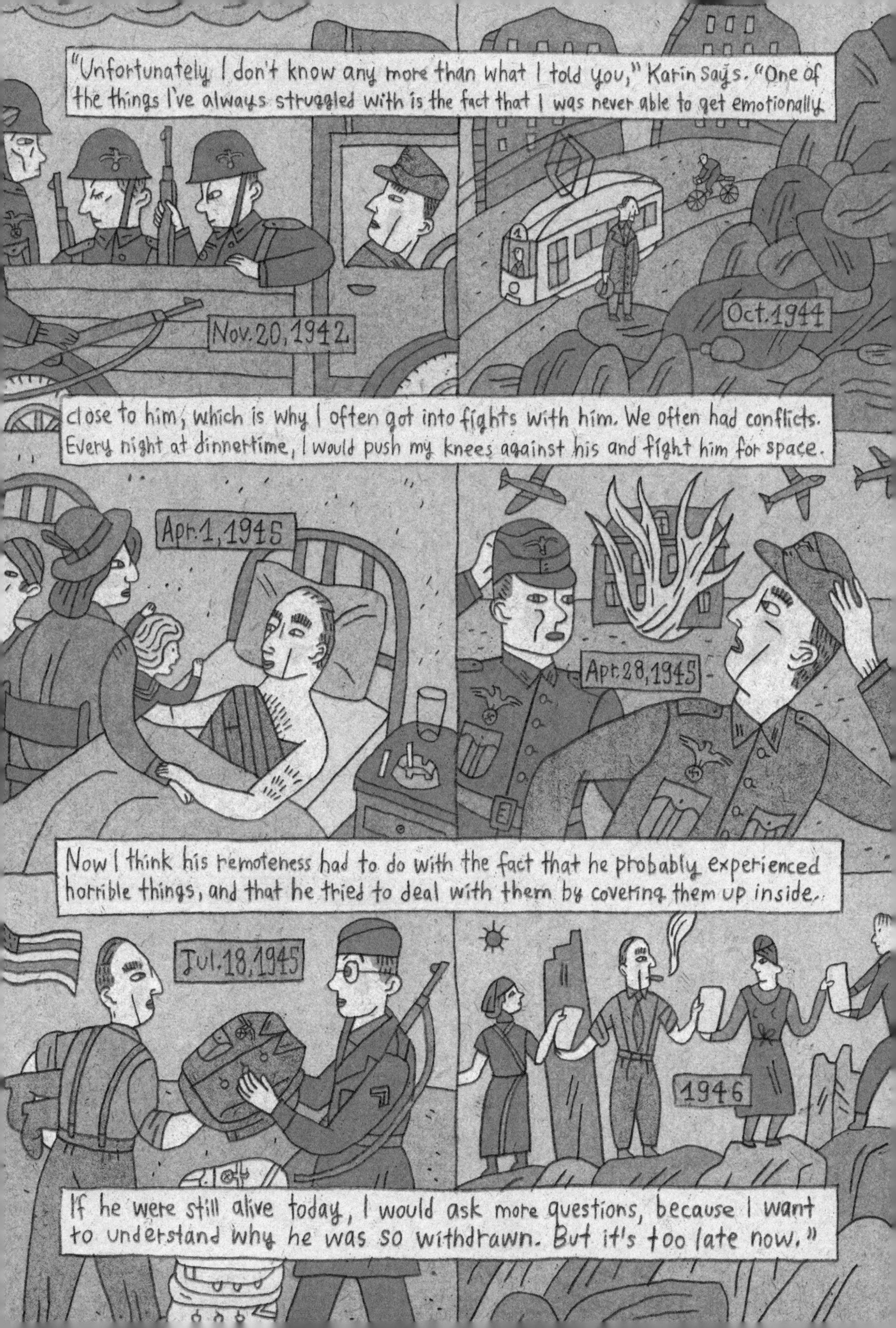
"Unfortunately I don't know any more than what I told you," Karin says. "One of the things I've always struggled with is the fact that I was never able to get emotionally
Nov. 20, 1942
Oct. 1944
close to him, which is why I often got into fights with him. We often had conflicts. Every night at dinnertime, I would push my knees against his and fight him for space.
Apr. 1, 1945
Apr. 28, 1945
Now I think his remoteness had to do with the fact that he probably experienced horrible things, and that he tried to deal with them by covering them up inside.
Jul. 18, 1945
1946
If he were still alive today, I would ask more questions, because I want to understand why he was so withdrawn. But it's too late now."

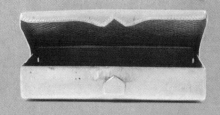

a. Tobacco case made by prisoner of war out of metal of crashed plane: €5

"Jebe"
NOTIZ-KALENDER
1 Woche auf einer Seite
1944
Ausgabe A

September

September

1939 Kriegserkl. Engl. u. Frankr.

Sonntag 10
Montag 11
Dienstag 12
Mittwoch 13
Donnerstag 14
Freitag 15
Sam./Sonn. 16

b. Soldier's calendar marking arrival at Stalingrad prisoner-of-war camp on Sept. 14 : €3

c. Postcard from International Red Cross to prisoner of war: €.20

"Your relatives have been without a sign of life from you for some time and are longing to hear from you."

CPOT DE PRISONNIERS DE GUERRE
Kriegsgefangenenlager

Date : 5. X. 1946
Datum :

d. Postcard from prisoner of war: €.20

"I had hoped that you'd think of me and write more often. ...I am still 38 pounds underweight."

Pforzheimerstrasse 43
14 a Mühlacker
Kr. Vaihingen / Württ.

la priant de vous transmettre le message suivant :

MESSAGE : Ihre Angehörigen sind seit längerer Zeit ohne ein Lebenszeichen von Ihnen und wünschen sehnlichst Nachrichten zu erhalten.

Date : 4.9.46

Prière de répondre à l'AGENCE CENTRALE DES PRISONNIERS DE GUERRE À GENÈVE, en utilisant la carte ci-dessous. Cependant si vous le désirez, vous pouvez écrire aussi directement à la personne sus-indiquée.

# 7.
## CLOSING IN

The closest I ever came to Külsheim as a child was when my father occasionally took us to visit his parents' grave on the outskirts of the town, an hour and a half away from Karlsruhe, where my parents still live. One day, he stopped the car at the town's entrance and turned to me and my brother.

"See that street back there? That's where I grew up. And see the house over there? That's where your aunt lives."

My brother and I got out of the car and entered the unfamiliar town. As if to ward off evil, we tread on the pavement as softly as we could. As we reached my aunt Annemarie's house, the door opened and a young woman appeared. I looked at her, curiously. She looked at me indifferently. I knew that my aunt had a daughter and a son, whom my father hadn't seen since they were children. Here was my cousin, and I didn't even know her name. We hurried back to the car and left the town where our family had lived for generations.

"Annemarie is the only person who can tell you anything," my father said whenever I asked about my uncle. "She has most of his photographs, too."

I asked my father why his relationship to Annemarie had disintegrated. "She was mean to me," he said in the scratchy voice he uses to conceal his anguish and suggested that we change the subject, and I could sense that he was deeply hurt.

For many years, I fantasized about ways that I could meet Annemarie.

I would ring the pretense public survey. that I came a documentary of Külsheim. tell her the that I was niece, who curiosity about whose loss is fabric of our

her bell under of conducting a I would claim to town to shoot about the history Or I would just truth and say her estranged had an insatiable her dead brother, part of the common history.

But I never returned to Külsheim and rang her bell.

Now, almost 30 years later, Annemarie is in her 80s.

If I don't break the silence, the memory of my uncle
Franz-karl will die with her. And with his memory buried,
how can I understand the meaning of my history?

I find the email address of Annemarie's son, Michael, on the website of
his veterinary clinic and write to him. The next day, I receive a response.

He was surprised to receive my email. He didn't know I existed. He remembers
my father vividly as the uncle who fed him mashed bananas with oatmeal
and sugar, which he still likes to eat. He and his family have often
talked about my father but never had the the courage to
contact him. He thinks that the idea of meeting as a new,
impartial generation
is a good one.

I am exhilarated.

I expect my father to be surprised when I tell him that I am planning to return to Külsheim.

Instead, he offers to drive me.

As we near his old HEIMAT, I roll down the windows to let in the summer air. Now it's just him and me and the chirping of the grasshoppers in the passing fields.

"Did you grow up feeling guilty about Germany's past?" I ask.
"No. I just felt terrified at the thought of what people are capable of doing to one another."

"When did you first realize that Külsheim has a Jewish history?"
"Only really when you started asking me about it."

"Did your mother talk about Külsheim's Jews?"
"Only once. She talked about a Jewish man who went from farm to farm to buy horses before the war. People said he cheated farmers into selling too cheaply. She also told me not to play at the Jewish cemetery, but I couldn't figure out why."

My father chooses every word carefully, as if this is the first time he has ever talked about these memories.

"Did nobody ever talk to you about what happened to the Jews in town?"

His voice sounds almost mechanical:
"There was no memory of Jewish people in Külsheim."

a. Adolf Hitler stamp, labeled "Germany's Contaminator" in purple by Allies

(possible counterfeit) : €4

b. Savings-bank account card with Allied-censored swastika : €.20

c. Incomplete photo album (incriminating pictures likely removed after 1945) : €8

d. Photograph with scratched-out swastikas : €.50

We pass through village after village, by the white-plastered houses with their pink geraniums, by deserted, centuries-old but modern-looking squares.

We pass by the village of Wenkheim — where a retired pig farmer volunteers as a guide to the renovated synagogue, whose new floors were made out of trees felled in a nearby forest by the men in town as an act of atonement — and by the village of Uissigheim — where the main street is named Ritter Arnold, after the medieval knight who killed Külsheim's Jews, whose gravestone is still displayed at the local church, worn by hundreds of years of worship (its dust was once used to treat diseased cattle).

"Why didn't you ever ask your mother about the war?" I ask my father.

"I don't know." His foot is shaking on the gas pedal.

"Don't you think it's a little odd that you never asked?"

"I felt no physical connection to the war. The only family members who were directly affected by it were my father and my brother, and I never got to know either of them."

We pass by the grotto with the well that spews holy water at the push of a button, and by the JÜDEKÄF, the piece of land still named after the centuries-old cemetery where Jews were once buried.

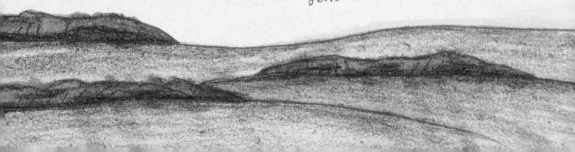

"I believe the green patch over there is land I inherited,"
my father says, and points at a field in the distance.

"What grows there?"
"Plum trees. And there's a little forest there, too."
"Wouldn't you want to visit it sometime?"

The grasshoppers have fallen silent.

"Wouldn't you want to visit it sometime?" I repeat.
"What for?!"
"It's your HEIMAT, after all!"
"These few plum trees aren't my HEIMAT."
"What is your HEIMAT, then?"
"I don't know. HEIMAT is a small, defined space, where you
feel comfortable," he says, as if quoting from a dictionary.
"Külsheim used to be my HEIMAT."

We merge onto the road to Külsheim that is lined with medieval
shrines of eternally suffering Jesuses.

"Why is your foot shaking," I ask.
"I don't know."
"Is it nervousness?"
"Perhaps."

Or is it just genetic? His mother's hands used
to shake like this when she got older, he once told me.

# 8.
# FATHOMLESS
# FORESTS

a. Letter containing lock of hair, dated 11/26/44: €.20

"The party is in full swing, ignore the spelling mistakes, I've had some wine. ...I'm the only one among the 24 of us who's writing a letter right now. ...My dear wifey, I feel a particular home-sickness for you right now. ...Well, how is our dear little Wolfgang ?? I could cry out loud when I look at his picture. ...Oh, the wine!"

c. Dried Edelweiss flower: €2

b. Letter dated 09/17/40 : €.20

"Because of our attacks on London, you'll probably be flooded with bombs earlier than expected. ...Just imagine: the war will end soon, we'll be victors all along the line, all kinds of fortunes will pour into the Reich, everything will blossom ... why shouldn't the two of us get some of it, too ?"

Willi's photographs, his uniform, his pay book, and his postcard book
from Flanders revealed some facts about his life, but little about his feelings.
     I need to dig deeper, search for more clues to my family's past.

     Karin has become as enthusiastic as I am about learning more.
     She contacts the granddaughter of Willi's brother, Edwin, in
     Switzerland — my distant cousin Sabine, whom I only met once,
when I was a child — to ask about the letters Edwin wrote
          to his family from the front line every other day.
A few weeks later, a package arrives in Brooklyn,
     containing 55 letters and a note from Sabine:
     "I hope this package includes what you're looking for."
          The letters are written in Sütterlin, the old black-letter
               handwriting, unintelligible to most modern German readers.

So I ask the help of a group of men and women at a nursing
     home in Germany, old enough to still be literate in Sütterlin, and
          send them Edwin's letters. During my next visit to Germany,
               I travel to the suburbs of Hamburg, to meet them.

     We gather in a meticulously tidy common room with tall windows.
     The sky is a dense mass of gray. Rain snakes down the panes.
"Some of the letters brought back dark memories," the man
who transcribed most of them tells me with a shaky voice,
     and his gaze turns inward, toward his childhood self that stole
coal briquettes from passing trains with frost-stiffened fingers.

The coal thief hands me a CD with Edwin's transcribed letters.

As I insert the CD into my computer, I can't shake the old familiar feeling: that I have no right to feel sad over the wartime loss of a German life. As I open the letters one by one, I am determined not to feel pity. I shield myself from tales of courage and camaraderie. But Edwin's letters to his wife, Elsa, adorned with drawings and pressed leaves and flowers, with place names censored by the military, sent from what he describes as the land of "fathomless forests, swamps, and steppes," chronicle nothing but his gradual emotional disintegration.

The East, May 23rd, 1944 When time allows it, I look at the little photos you've sent. Each time I find something new and magnetic about them. This pocket album is my sanctuary because I have nothing else of you. Just my thoughts which are always with you. The East, June 2nd, 1944 There is a song that says, "I keep on thinking about how wonderful it is to be a soldier." But for me it's just the opposite. I keep on thinking how wonderful it would be to be home. The East, June 8th, 1944 Our separation has curbed my appetite. I have to take my belt in two holes, and I realize I can't go on like this, or I'll get ill.

The East, June 27th, 1944 I've never seen a sunrise in my life as beautiful as the one I saw this morning. A narrow strip of cloud covered the horizon that looked like liquid precious metal. Nature's gift is the only good thing at these difficult times. If we didn't have that, what would we do, we little human beings? The East, August 11th, 1944 My longing for you will soon suffocate my heart. ██████, September 6th, 1944 I had hoped I could help you with the harvest this fall, but even this hope has dwindled. Isn't it true, Elsa, that if you plant

something and you can protect and foster it until it's ripe, you develop a certain love for it, without which nothing can prosper? When you write about the children I'm so happy, and I am confirmed in thinking that there is a purpose to life. I'm here for someone I can care for, you and I. ██████, October 17th, 1944 Dear Elsa, I'm grateful that I can write at all, because what lies behind me isn't easy, and even if I return home, I'll never forget it. You pickled vegetables for me in the basement. But whether I'll get to have them only time will tell. If it continues the way it is now, there is no hope for keeping up.

, October 31st, 1944  A wind blows across the narrow strip of land that goes right to the core and makes your limbs freeze. What the war expects of us goes far beyond the superhuman in all respects. , November 9th, 1944 My longing for you is almost making me sick. On October 8th, we ran after the Russians for altogether 32 hours. One day this war has to end. The piece of land where I lie now is just 3 kilometers wide. We're a good target for the enemy, and he for us, because neither of us can go any further from here.

, November 13th, 1944  Yesterday was Sunday, and I was thinking of you even in the early morning hours. I remembered the time when the two of us went into the woods together, and when we collected things from the forest. I've seen some wonderful chanterelles, but what good are they if you don't get a chance to cook them? Slowly, the berries and mushrooms are coming to an end, because nature is beginning to show its cold face. Everything dies or, better, returns to its inner calm. Even humans long for that, but unfortunately it isn't possible in these eventful times. Now the truck is arriving and I have to stop writing.

At the front line, December 28th, 1944

Dear Ms. Rock,

I'm sorry to let you know that your husband, Private Edwin Rock, did not return to his company after combat on the peninsula of Sworbe on November 18th, 1944, and has been missing since.

Immediate investigation of your husband's whereabouts have remained inconclusive so far, and no clarification was gained by inquiring with the other members of his company. The company will inform you immediately upon learning more about your husband's fate. May the knowledge that his mission was dedicated to the struggle for the freedom of his HEIMAT give you strength to bear your pain.


      Heil Hitler!
      The Captain and Company Leader

Finally, my emotions catch up with me.
For the first time, I feel my family's loss.

And through this loss,
I feel the gap between me and Willi shrink.

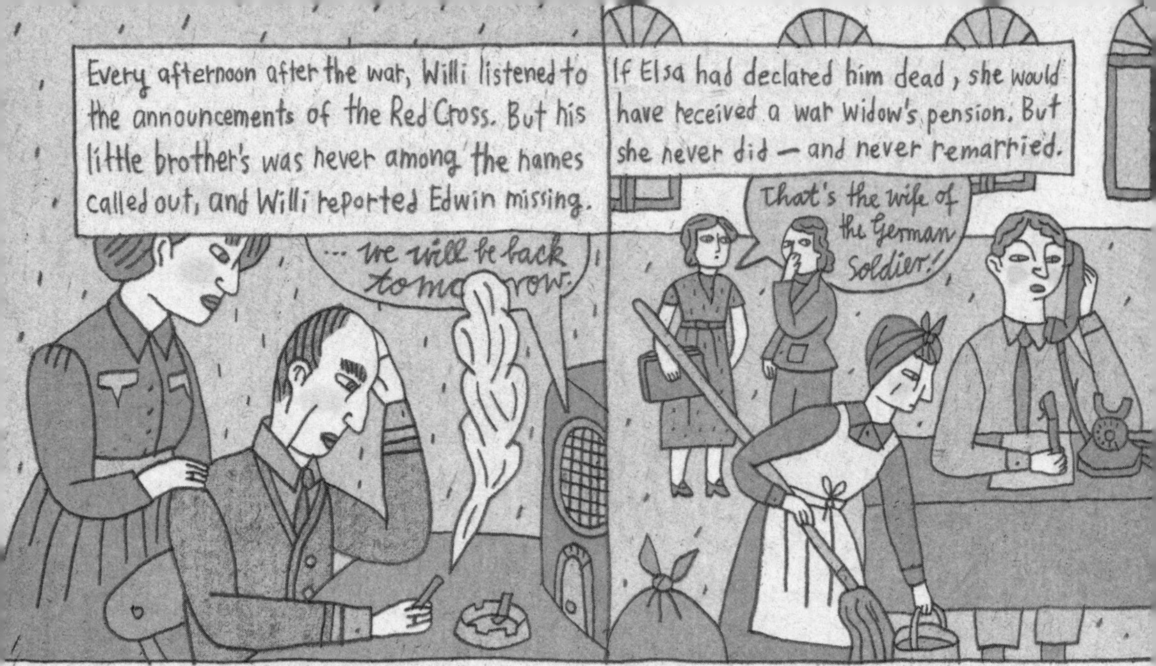
Every afternoon after the war, Willi listened to the announcements of the Red Cross. But his little brother's was never among the names called out, and Willi reported Edwin missing.
... we will be back tomo[...]row.
If Elsa had declared him dead, she would have received a war widow's pension. But she never did — and never remarried.
That's the wife of the German soldier!

In 2009, one hundred years after Edwin was born, his grandchildren received a letter from the German Red Cross:

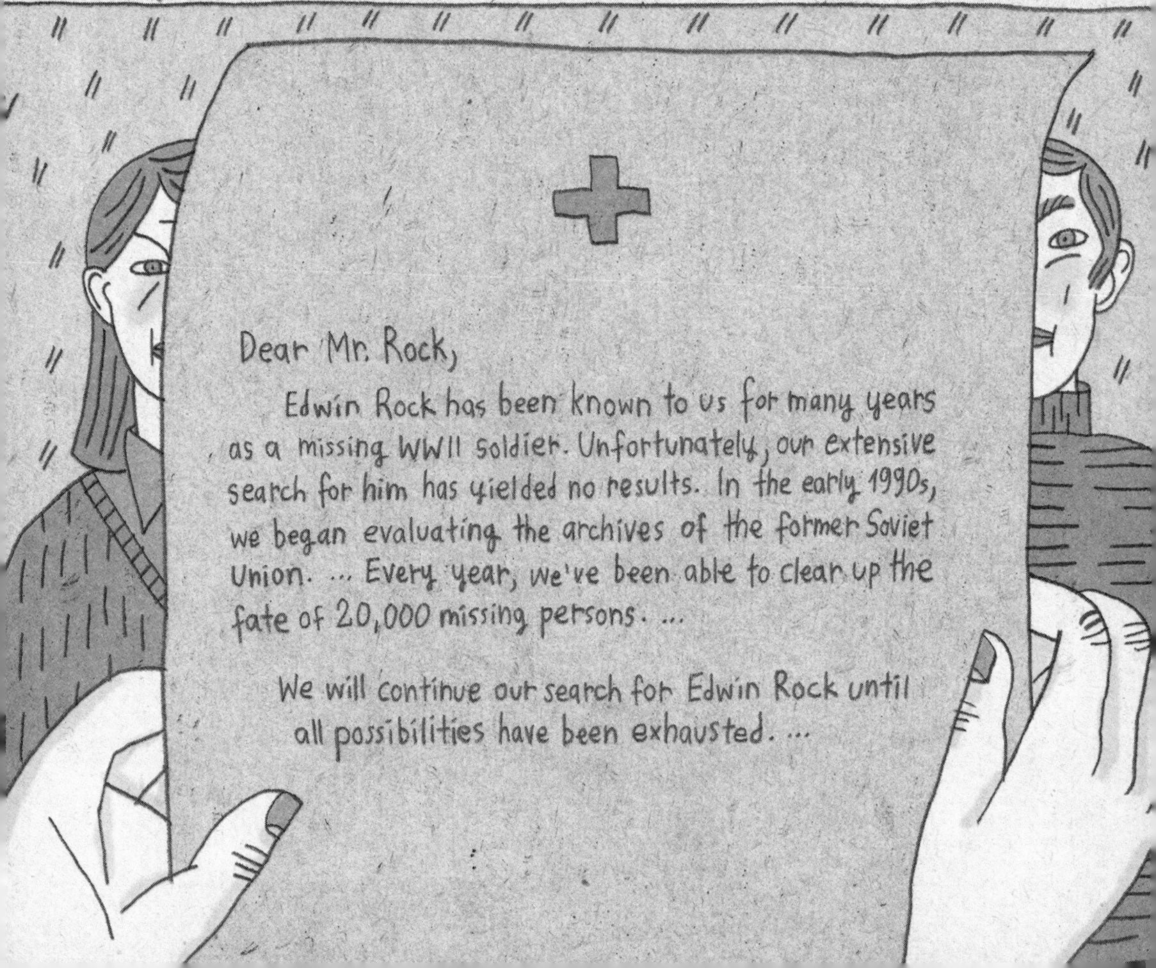
Dear Mr. Rock,
Edwin Rock has been known to us for many years as a missing WWII soldier. Unfortunately, our extensive search for him has yielded no results. In the early 1990s, we began evaluating the archives of the former Soviet Union. ... Every year, we've been able to clear up the fate of 20,000 missing persons. ...
We will continue our search for Edwin Rock until all possibilities have been exhausted. ...

9.
MELTING
ICE

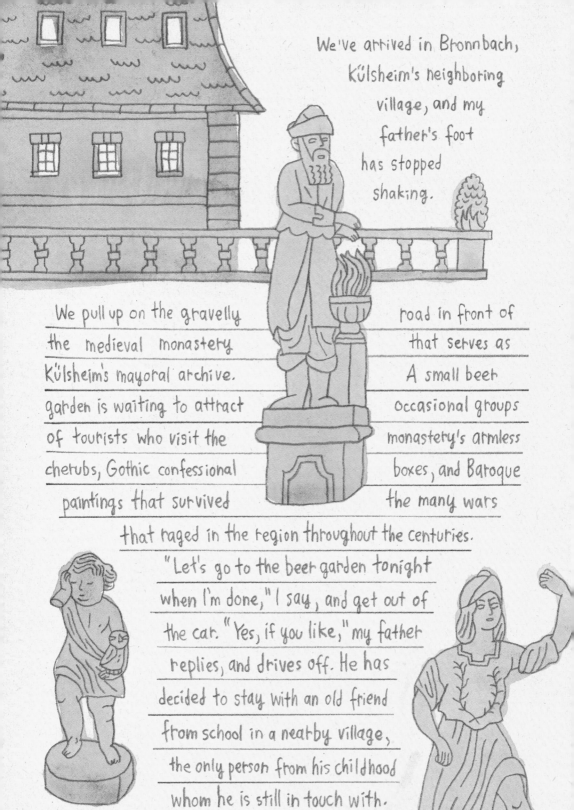

We've arrived in Bronnbach, Külsheim's neighboring village, and my father's foot has stopped shaking.

We pull up on the gravelly road in front of the medieval monastery that serves as Külsheim's mayoral archive. A small beer garden is waiting to attract occasional groups of tourists who visit the monastery's armless cherubs, Gothic confessional boxes, and Baroque paintings that survived the many wars that raged in the region throughout the centuries.

"Let's go to the beer garden tonight when I'm done," I say, and get out of the car. "Yes, if you like," my father replies, and drives off. He has decided to stay with an old friend from school in a nearby village, the only person from his childhood whom he is still in touch with.

> I enter the archive's reading room and find it filled with documents relating to the war: binders packed with letters, files and files of paper conversations.

## Fragebogen zur Dokumentation der Judenschicksale

Gemeinde: K ü l s h e i m          Kreis: Tauberbischofsheim

From the mayor of K. to the director of the Stuttgart Archive, 10/04/1963

Re: Documentation of the fate of the Jews, in response to your letters.

I'm attaching the completed questionnaire regarding the fate of the Jews. We have interviewed many of our town's older residents so that the questionnaire could be filled out in a reasonable manner.

4. Spielten die Juden im öffentlichen Leben der Gemeinde vor 1933 eine Rolle (als Gemeinderat, Bürgermeister, Gemeindebedienstete, Mitglieder politischer Parteien, Mitglieder von Vereinen usw.)?

Samuel Scheuer war von 1933 als Gemeinderat tätig

#16 What was the relationship like between Jews and Christians in town?

    Normal.

a) eigene Schulen (welche)?     nein

#17 What effect did Nazi propaganda have on the relationship between Jews and Christians?

    People didn't take much notice of it and continued buying quite a few things from them.

#20 In what way were Jews assaulted?

    The Jews were all put under house arrest for about 6 weeks, they were only allowed to leave the house at certain hours in order to go shopping.

g) ein Krankenhaus?         nein

#21 Was an official boycott against Jewish businesses instigated on April 1st, 1933?

    No.

i) ein Waisenhaus?          nein

#23 Were Jewish people attacked as a result of REICHSKRISTALLNACHT in 1938?

    No.

6. Sind Stiftungen von Juden zu allgemeinen karitativen Zwecken, zur Förderung von Kunst und Wissenschaft bekannt?     nein

— 6 —

34. Welche Einwohner der Gemeinde standen mit Juden in geschäftlicher Verbindung?

#29 Did an intervention take place against those who bought from Jews, those who protected Jews, and those who protested against arbitrary actions?

No.

35. Welche Einwohner waren bei Juden beschäftigt? Welche von ihnen leben noch?

#30 Were National Socialists who engaged in offenses against Jews or damaged or destroyed Jewish property prosecuted after the war?

No.

36. Wie lange durften Nichtjuden in Haushalten und Betrieben von Juden arbeiten?

seit ca 1930 waren keine Nichtjuden mehr bei Juden im Haushalt beschäftigt

#38 How were Jewish schoolchildren treated by their fellow pupils?

Well.

hier
gut

39. Wurden in der Gemeinde zu Anfang des Krieges die Juden in besondere Judenhäuser umquartiert bzw. zusammengelegt?

ja

#41 How did the deportation take place?

The people were loaded onto a lorry and brought to an unknown place.

41. Wie gingen die Deportationen vor sich?

Die Leuten wurden auf einen Lastwagen aufgeladen und weggefahren nach unbekannt.

#48 Is there a synagogue?

No. The synagogue was sold on January 12, 1940, to a neighbor by the people in power. The neighbor, a farmer, used the building as a storage room for his agricultural machines. In 1944, a fire, caused by a short circuit in the barn, destroyed the barn and the synagogue. The insurance company accepted the claim.

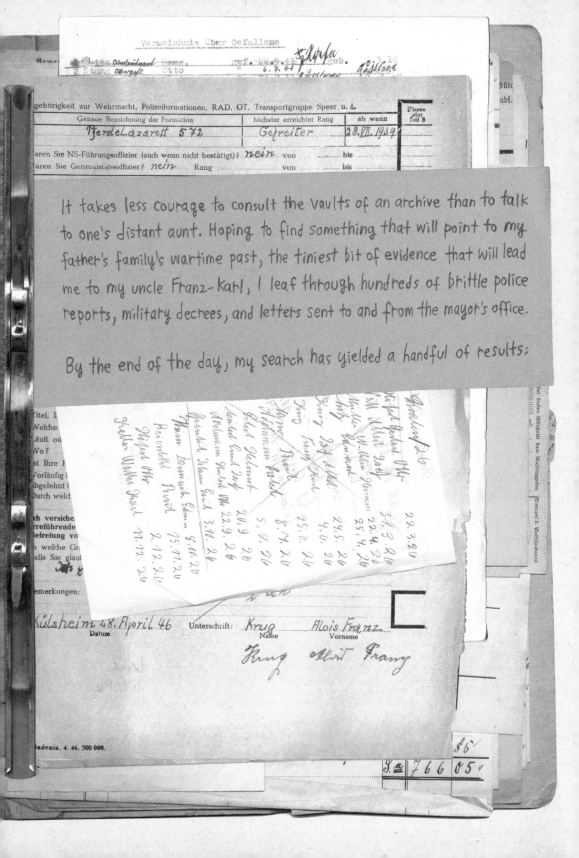

gehörigkeit zur Wehrmacht, Polizeiformationen, RAD, OT, Transportgruppe Speer u. &.

| Genaue Bezeichnung der Formation | höchster erreichter Rang | ab wann | Klasse oder Teil B |
|---|---|---|---|
| PferdeLazarett 572 | Gefreiter | 28.VII.1939 | |

Waren Sie NS-Führungsoffizier (auch wenn nicht bestätigt)? nein von ... bis ...

Waren Sie Generalstabsoffizier? nein Rang ... von ... bis ...

It takes less courage to consult the vaults of an archive than to talk to one's distant aunt. Hoping to find something that will point to my father's family's wartime past, the tiniest bit of evidence that will lead me to my uncle Franz-Karl, I leaf through hundreds of brittle police reports, military decrees, and letters sent to and from the mayor's office.

By the end of the day, my search has yielded a handful of results:

Titel, ...
Welche ...
Läuft od...
Wo?
ist Ihre ...
Vorläufig ...
abgelehnt ...
Durch welch ...

ch versiche...
rreführende...
Befreiung vo...
n welche Gr...
alls Sie glaub...

Bemerkungen:

Külsheim 28. April 46   Unterschrift:   Krug      Alois Franz
Datum                                   Name       Vorname

Krug  Alois Franz

Badenia. 4. 46. 300 000.

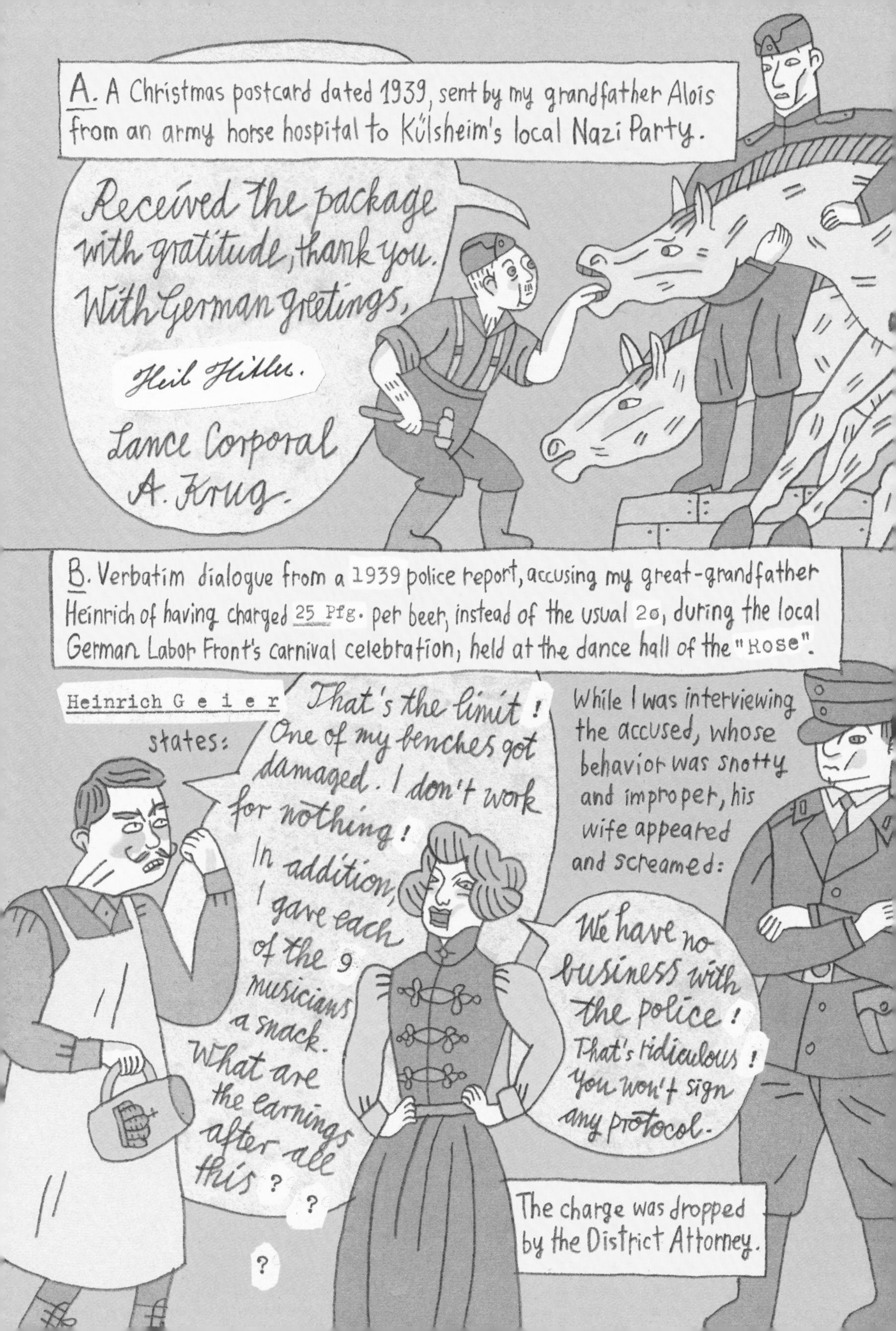
A. A Christmas postcard dated 1939, sent by my grandfather Alois from an army horse hospital to Külsheim's local Nazi Party.
Received the package with gratitude, thank you. With German greetings,
Heil Hitler.
Lance Corporal A. Krug.
B. Verbatim dialogue from a 1939 police report, accusing my great-grandfather Heinrich of having charged 25 Pfg. per beer, instead of the usual 20, during the local German Labor Front's carnival celebration, held at the dance hall of the "Rose".
Heinrich G e i e r states:
That's the limit! One of my benches got damaged. I don't work for nothing! In addition, I gave each of the 9 musicians a snack. What are the earnings after all this???
While I was interviewing the accused, whose behavior was snotty and improper, his wife appeared and screamed:
We have no business with the police! That's ridiculous! You won't sign any protocol.
The charge was dropped by the District Attorney.

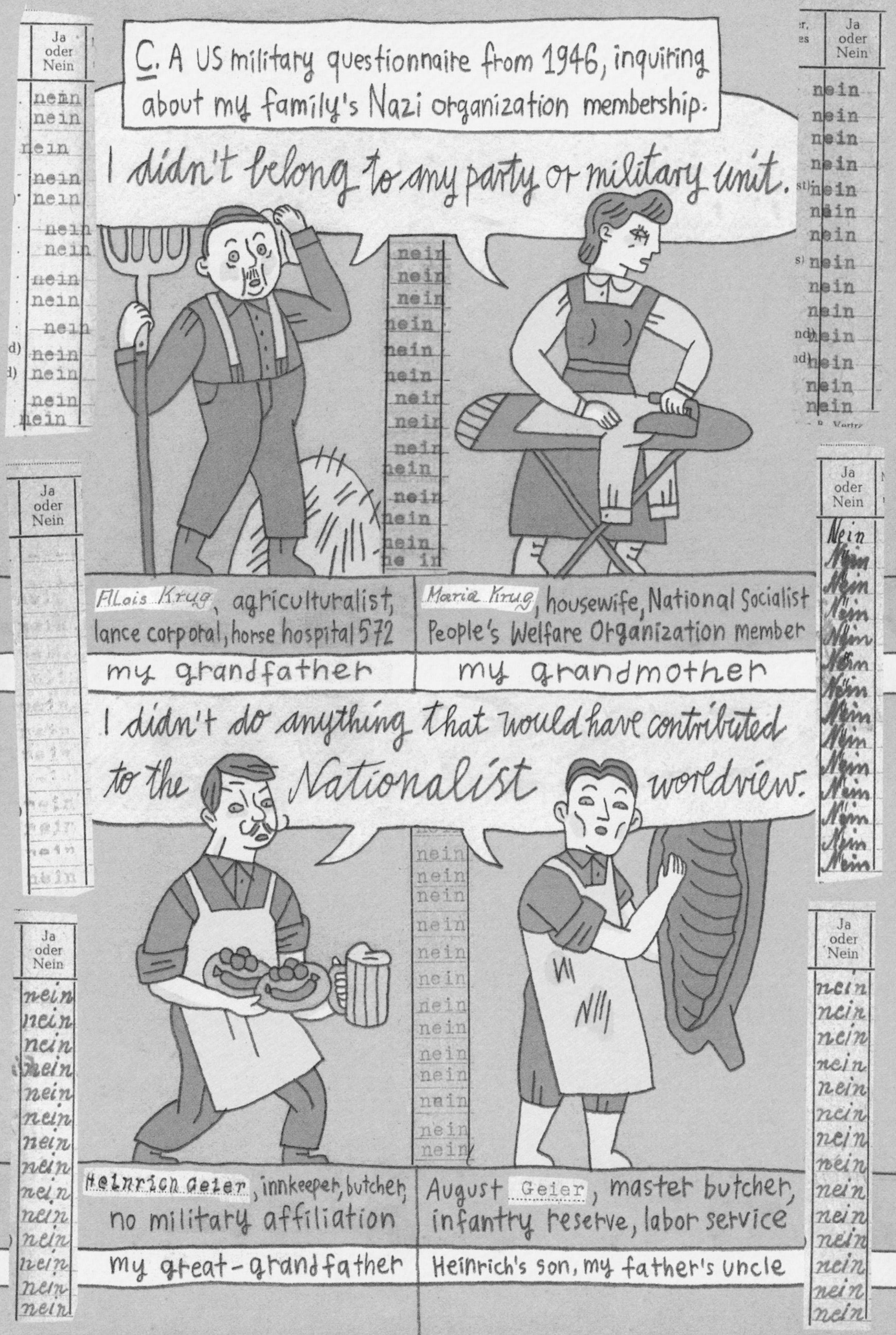

C. A US military questionnaire from 1946, inquiring about my family's Nazi organization membership.
I didn't belong to any party or military unit.
Alois Krug, agriculturalist, lance corporal, horse hospital 572
my grandfather
Maria Krug, housewife, National Socialist People's Welfare Organization member
my grandmother
I didn't do anything that would have contributed to the Nationalist worldview.
Heinrich Geier, innkeeper, butcher, no military affiliation
my great-grandfather
August Geier, master butcher, infantry reserve, labor service
Heinrich's son, my father's uncle
Ja oder Nein
nein

D. A handwritten response by the mayor to a 1941 request from the Ministry of the Interior for an index of all of Külsheim's boys born between 1924 and 1929, to confirm their membership in the _Hitler_ Youth, listing my uncle's name.

After all it's not our fault that my brother, who was a farmer and would be cultivating the land today, died in the last World War. We have to wait to cultivate the land until my (other) brother has grown up.

E. A 1940s index of Külsheim's "fallen soldiers." Erroneously, Russia is listed as my uncle Franz-Karl's place of death.

F. A letter written by my aunt Annemarie in 1961, in response to a request by the district office for the compulsory sale of farmland to be used as a military training ground. Annemarie agrees to the sale of the land, but asks to be compensated with the same fee as someone owning a working farm.

The rawness of her loss is palpable. And for a moment, I feel close to her.

Abschrift

ffmann                                         Kp.Gefechtsstand.22.VII.44
S Sturf.u.Kp.Chef
p.Nr.38030 C

G. A transcript of the letter my grandparents
received when Franz-Karl died in Italy.

Sehr geehrter Herr Krug !

Als Kompanie-Chef Jhres Sohnes, des SS-Ober-Grenadiers Franz Karl
Krug,geb. 4.6.26  habe ich die traurige Pflicht Sie von seinem
Heldentod in Kenntnis zu setzen.

Jhr Sohn wurde bei der Abwehr eines feindlichen Angriffes bei
Fauglin ( Jtalien), in vordester Linie der Kompanie durch einen
Brustschuß  tödlich getroffen.

Dear Mr. Krug!

As company commander of your son, SS senior infantryman
Franz-karl krug, born June 4th, 1926, I have the sad
duty to inform you of his heroic death.

Your son was killed by a shot in the chest while
fending off an enemy attack at the company's front
rank near Fauglia (Italy).

His comrades had grown deeply fond of him, of his vigor
and daredevil youthfulness. As a soldier and a man of
the SS, he fought, weapon in hand, till the bitter end.

You and your good wife can be quite proud of your son.
May his life and his heroic death serve as a small
consolation to this great pain. In remembrance of your
son, I send you greetings in the name of my company,
which will treasure the memory of SS senior infantryman
Franz-Karl krug in all eternity.


Heil Hitler!

Yours, Hoffmann
SS Assault Leader

A letter equal in kindness and in cruelty.

Its message strikes me to the core.

The letter describes the last moment of my uncle's life, the very moment I had tried to imagine when standing at his grave in Italy.

Here is my uncle, frozen in time.

Picturing the moment of his death brings me closer than ever to him.

"Dreadful" is all my father says when I show him a scan of the letter. We are the only customers at the beer garden that night.

My father's cousin Emilia was there the day the letter was delivered.

"I was with Annemarie at your grand-parents' farm. Alois was pacing the yard.

He was agitated and looked distraught. He pressed his hands against his cheeks.

A few years ago, after several decades of silence, she called my father out of the blue from Bondurant, Iowa (where she relocated

'What's wrong with you?' I asked him. 'Do you have a toothache?'

He just stood there and said nothing and stared into the distance.

after falling in love with an American GI), to touch base. A few weeks after my visit to the archive, I call her and ask what she remembers.

Then he went inside the house and told Maria that their son was dead.

Maria cried out loudly and collapsed onto the floor."

As she speaks, the past reveals itself as if through a block of melting ice.

"Maria later said that she had had a premonition," Emilia says, "a dream in which her son appeared to her and told her he was dead."

# 10.
# LOOKING
# FOR TRACES

# FROM THE SCRAPBOOK OF A MEMORY ARCHIVIST

## Flea market find # 6 : *Soldiers at Play*

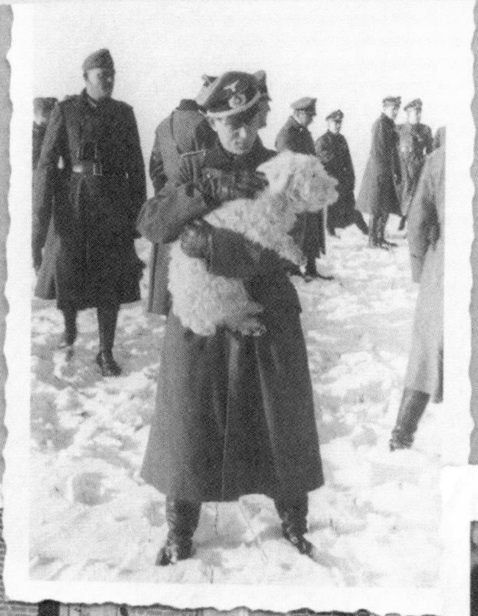

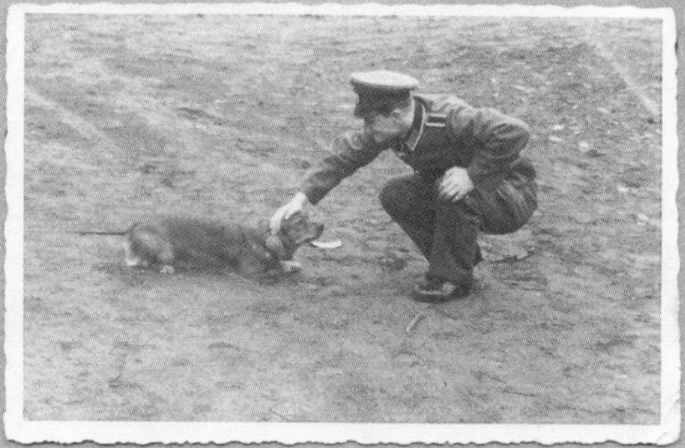

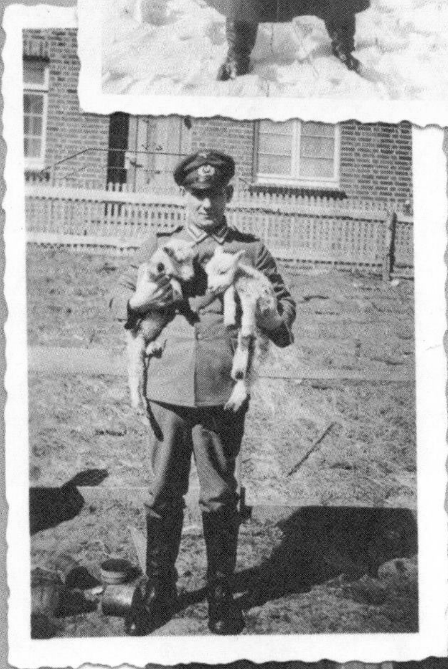

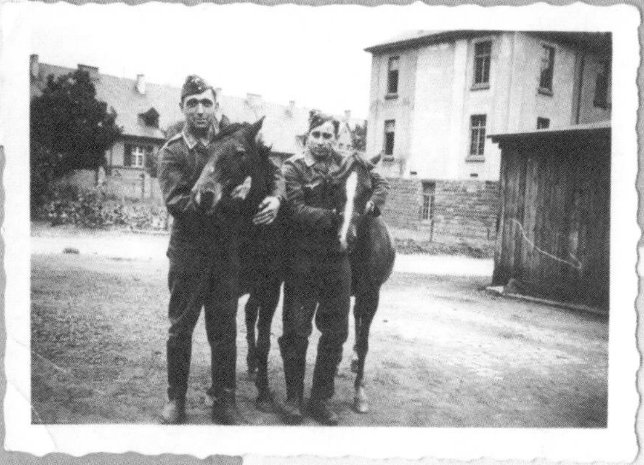

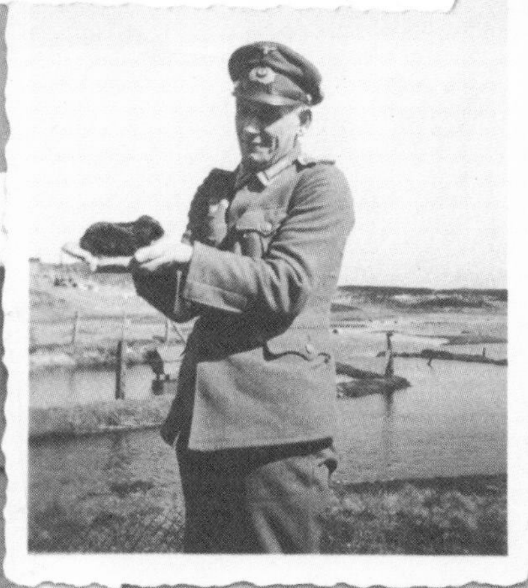

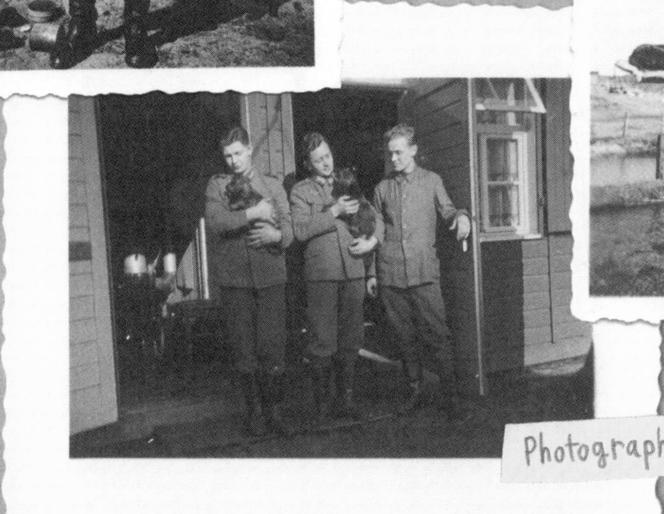

Photographs : €.50 – €1 each

"I'm convinced that Willi was no perpetrator," my mother tells me during my next visit to Karlsruhe. We're in the kitchen and she is cooking eggs with fried potatoes and Black Forest Speck in a cast-iron pan. It's been over twenty years since I asked her anything about her father.

"He never spoke  about politics in a fanatical way. 'Politics is a dirty business,' he used to say, and that it is better to avoid conflict. And he was softhearted. He would never have beaten us, or anything like that." She rubs her hands dry on her apron.

Willi and Karin, 1941

"How did he respond when you confronted him about the war?" I ask. "He said he never held a gun in his hands. I told my parents that there isn't such a thing as being apolitical and asked why they hadn't been in the resistance. They said it would have been too dangerous, with a little child and all. I'm sure, though, that if they had been Nazi supporters, they would have tried to make the regime look less negative in hindsight. I felt no need to check whether what they said was true."

Perhaps it is because I never had the chance to ask my grandparents directly that I need stronger proof than my mother did.

It is my mother who suggests that I visit Karlsruhe's archive and ask about Willi's US military file — one of the many thousands containing information about the wartime past of Germans, released and made accessible not long ago.

Anyone can request their family members' files.
She read about it in the local paper.

I have to take a detour to the archive because another undetonated WWII bomb was recently discovered during the construction of a new shopping center.

I ride my bike down the street where the Nazis marched by torchlight; make a right on the plaza where thousands gathered to support the boycott of Jewish shops; and arrive at the street where a group of Social Democrats — members of the leftist party that opposed the Nazi regime — were escorted from prison to police headquarters in a public parade, and from there to Kislau, a nearby concentration camp.

Ludwig Marum

The prisoners upon their arrival at the camp.

That day in May 1933, only months after Adolf Hitler came to power, the sidewalks were lined with people. Party members squeezed through the crowds and handed out lyrics to Schubert's song "The Miller's Joy Is Wandering" because the captured "criminal rogues" were also about to wander off toward an uncertain destination. Swollen with confidence, the crowd sang full throated along with the accompanying brass band.

Ludwig Marum, a Jewish lawyer who was among the arrested, wrote to his wife from the camp: "I rule out Palestine as an option, because I don't feel an inner connection to Judaism, even though I've never denied my heritage. Germany is my HEIMAT and I will cling to it." About six months later, Marum was strangled to death in his cell by order of the GAULEITER (local party leader), Robert Wagner: "Suicide in a fit of dejection." Crowds of men and women came to pay their respects when his body was laid out at the local cemetery. Thousands attended his cremation.

Did Willi take part in the parade? Or did he attend the funeral? He used to tell my mother that he had always voted for the Social Democrats.

# Local election results, March 1933 (voter participation 88%):

Was Willi among the 17,886 who voted for the Social Democrats?

In the subsequent 1938 election, the local Nazi Party reported that 99.53 of every 100 men and women in town voted for Adolf Hitler. How likely is it that Willi was among those who didn't?

"I'm looking for US military files on my grandfather." I feel as if I were at the doctor's office, asking to be tested for a rare genetic disease. "Lots of people come by to ask," the archivist reassures me.

In order to "free Germany from National Socialism and militarism," the US army issued a questionnaire to every adult living in the US sector, designed to evaluate their political involvement under the Nazi regime. Based on the questionnaire, 13 million Germans were ranked into five categories for prosecution purposes: 1.9% were categorized as Exonerated Persons, 51.1% as Followers, 11.2% as Lesser Offenders, and 2.5% combined as Offenders and Major Offenders, Thirty-three percent of all charges were dropped.

The archivist's fingers spell out Willi's name on the keyboard. "I myself just pulled up my grandfather's file and found out that he was in the SS." My short-lived reassurance dwindles.

My grandfather's name pops up on the screen like an alarming find on an X-ray image. "Yes, we do have a file on your grandfather. I'll let you know when it's ready for you to look at." I have to wait to find out if it's malignant or not.

The adjacent reading room is lined with Karlsruhe's phone books from 1890 to 1946. I am related by blood to some of the men and women who lie buried in these paper graveyards. Some of the names printed on these pages belonged to my grandfather's friends, neighbors, and colleagues. One of these men was his Jewish employer. But too many linen salesmen are listed under the "Dowry Laundry" section in the 1930 phone book for me to find him.

Gauleiter Robert Wagner M.d.R.
Reichsstatthalter von Baden

The 1933 phone book opens with a portrait of the local Nazi GAULEITER, Robert Wagner, a long-standing close ally of the Führer's. Willi must have owned a copy of this phone book, must have looked at the same frowning face I am looking at now.

I leaf through the phone books one by one and try to reconstruct the narrative of my grandfather's life.

Willi makes his first appearance, as a mechanic, in the 1930/31 edition.

In the 1933/34 volume, he is listed as a driving teacher.

By 1934/35, he owns his own driving school, located on Kaiserstraße, one of the main streets in town. If Willi started his driving school in 1933 or 1934, his Jewish employer must have given him the money in the early 1930s.

Nobody was hiding anyone in a shed as early as that.

For the first time, a telephone number is listed along with his address: 3935 Four simple digits, promising direct access to the past. What if I dialed this number now? Would I recognize the sound of his voice?

I inspect over 800 photographs taken in Karlsruhe between 1933 and 1945 on the archive's fuzzy computer screen. I look for Willi's lanky body, his sloping shoulders and curved nose among the crowds celebrating Adolf Hitler's birthday, among those waiting to salute the Führer in his passing car, and among the ones gathered to show their support for the boycott of Jewish shops.

I wait for him to turn around and look at me in the crowd that bellows out "The Miller's Joy Is Wandering," but there is no trace of Willi.

I unfold the crinkled map in the back of the 1938 volume,

run my finger down Kaiserstraße,

and stop at the rectangle that was Willi's driving school.

As I make out the tiny letters on the building directly across from the driving school, my lungs refuse to take in air:

the synagogue and its administrative building, the center of Karlsruhe's Jewish cultural life, were located right across from Willi's office.

"People back then weren't very political," Aunt Karin used to tell me. "They had many things to worry about. Women washed their laundry by hand back then! Men were worried about not being able to feed their families. I doubt that he even read the paper."

# Der Führer

From **Der Führer**,

Karlsruhe's local Nazi paper, November 10th, 1938:

"When it became known... that the assault on the German diplomat... von Rath by a murderous Jew resulted in deadly injuries, the rage of the past days boiled over and spontaneous demonstrations could not be avoided. ...During the course of yesterday morning, a large group of Jews were arrested and taken to the police station. This event was accompanied by cheering from the angry crowd that filled the streets around Adolf Hitler Square. ... A large group of these Jews will now have to leave town. ... Entering the Jews' houses during the arrests was enlightening: There were the Jewish money magnates with their feudal homes, with their silver, gold, and antique German art objects, amassed in greed; and then there were the Galicians with their greasy, bug-ridden, verminous junk stores. Both kinds were equally insolent during their arrest. They tried to... escape by coming up with all kinds of excuses. ... They tried to threaten, they pleaded in whiney tones, they put on submissive faces and acted as though they carried all of the world's pain on their shoulders. ..."

Even without reading the paper, Willi would have known what was going on the night of November 9 and 10, 1938, REICHSKRISTALLNACHT.

That night, the synagogue across from his office was set on fire by members of the "protection squadron," dressed in plainclothes.

The street index in the back of the 1938 phone book reveals that Willi's office was located on the second floor. He must have been able to see the synagogue and its administrative building through his second-floor window.

Even if he wasn't at his office when the synagogue was set ablaze, he must have noticed the burned-out building the next day.

And even if Anna was doing the laundry that day, there was no way he wouldn't have told her what he had seen or heard.

Robert Wagner, the Nazi with the frowning face, whose picture I saw in the 1933 phone book, had given orders to burn the synagogue and to keep the fire from spreading to a fuel depot that was located directly behind the synagogue.

## From a local firefighter's postwar account:

"Alarm was raised at about 10p.m. ... Naturally, the glow of the fire had attracted many people who stood around and watched. ... When we arrived at the synagogue, we noticed that fires had been laid throughout the building. The leader of our group shouted: 'This is church desecration!' He hadn't noticed the policemen and members of the 'assault division' in plainclothes standing nearby. The fire was duly extinguished. The damage was so minimal that after a half-hour cleanup, the synagogue was usable again. ... A day later, order was given to set the synagogue on fire a second time. But we are firemen, not arsonists, so the synagogue didn't burn again."

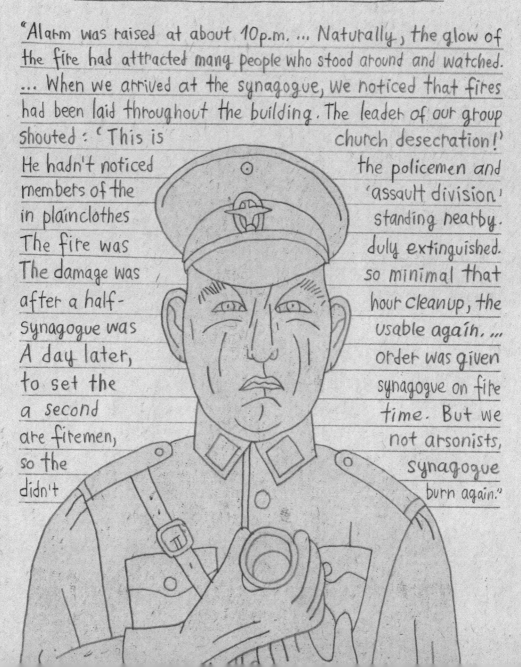

"We didn't sleep well that night. We heard sirens blaring, glass breaking, screaming, orders being shouted — I can still hear it now. The next morning, ...I ran through the streets full of curiosity and fear. ... I didn't understand what had happened. ... A large group of people stood in front of the synagogue, men from the 'protection squadron' carried out Torah scrolls and a smoldering. armchair and threw them on a pile. Most people soon lost interest, because there wasn't much else to see. ... Then I heard someone shout: 'There's Something happening at Adolf Hitler Square!' And a moment later, I was in the middle of a crowd streaming to the square. It was packed with people!"

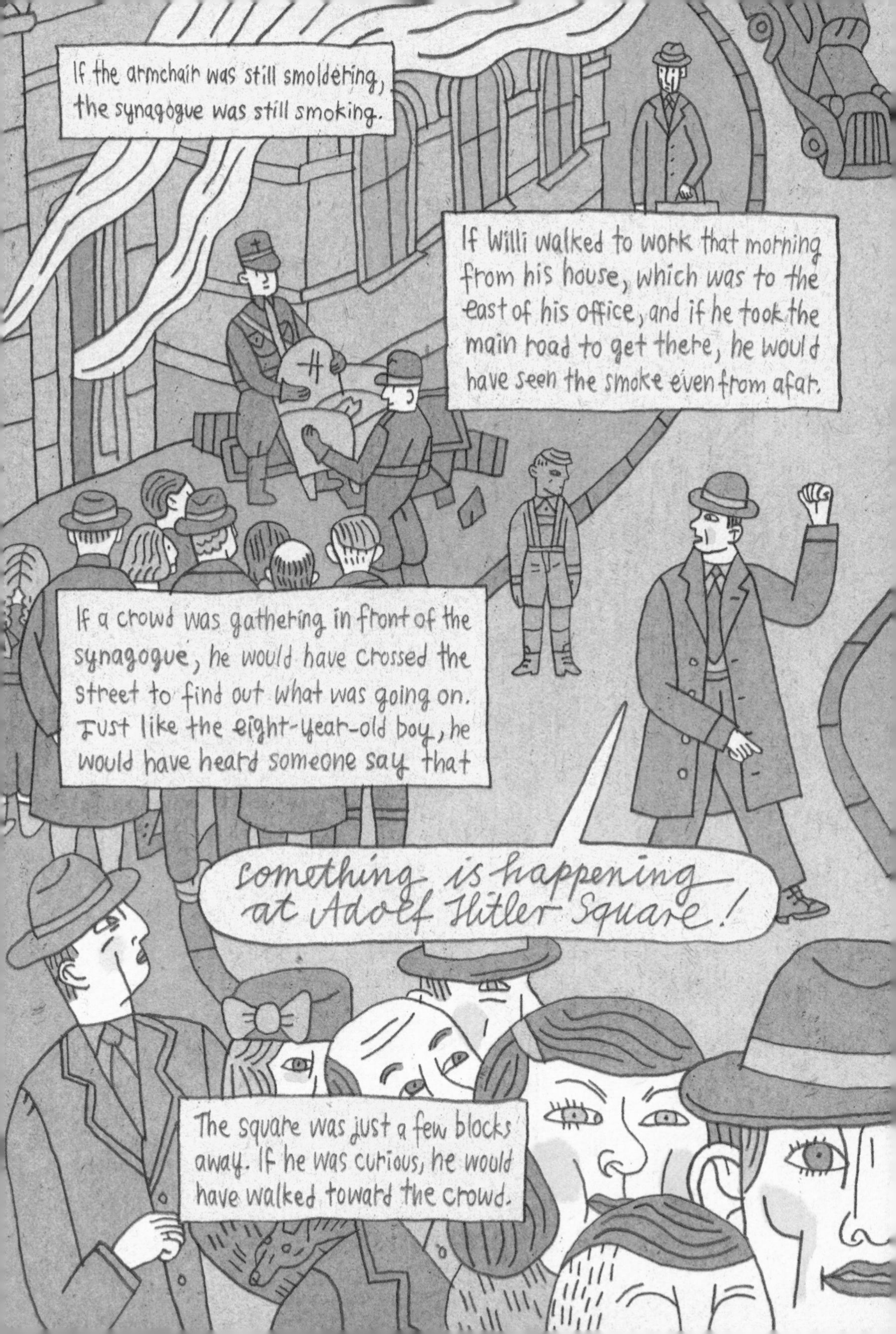
If the armchair was still smoldering, the synagogue was still smoking.
If Willi walked to work that morning from his house, which was to the east of his office, and if he took the main road to get there, he would have seen the smoke even from afar.
If a crowd was gathering in front of the synagogue, he would have crossed the street to find out what was going on. Just like the eight-year-old boy, he would have heard someone say that
Something is happening at Adolf Hitler Square!
The square was just a few blocks away. If he was curious, he would have walked toward the crowd.

# The man's account continues:

"There was tension in the air. ... Everything was terribly exciting, but also disturbing. ... I'd never heard such hooting before. I couldn't see what was going on. So I climbed up on the fountain in front of the town hall with a couple of other boys. And then I saw that several vans approached the square, packed with people. The people, who I later learned were Jews, were then pushed out of the vans and shoved toward

the police station.

... The crowd ... battered the Jews with their bags, sticks, and umbrellas and spat at them. I will never for- get a tall, old, and bald man with a long, gray beard who passed by night in front of me. Proud and erect, and with an expression of contempt, he walked toward the police station past the battering mob, his face covered with blood from several lacerations on his head."

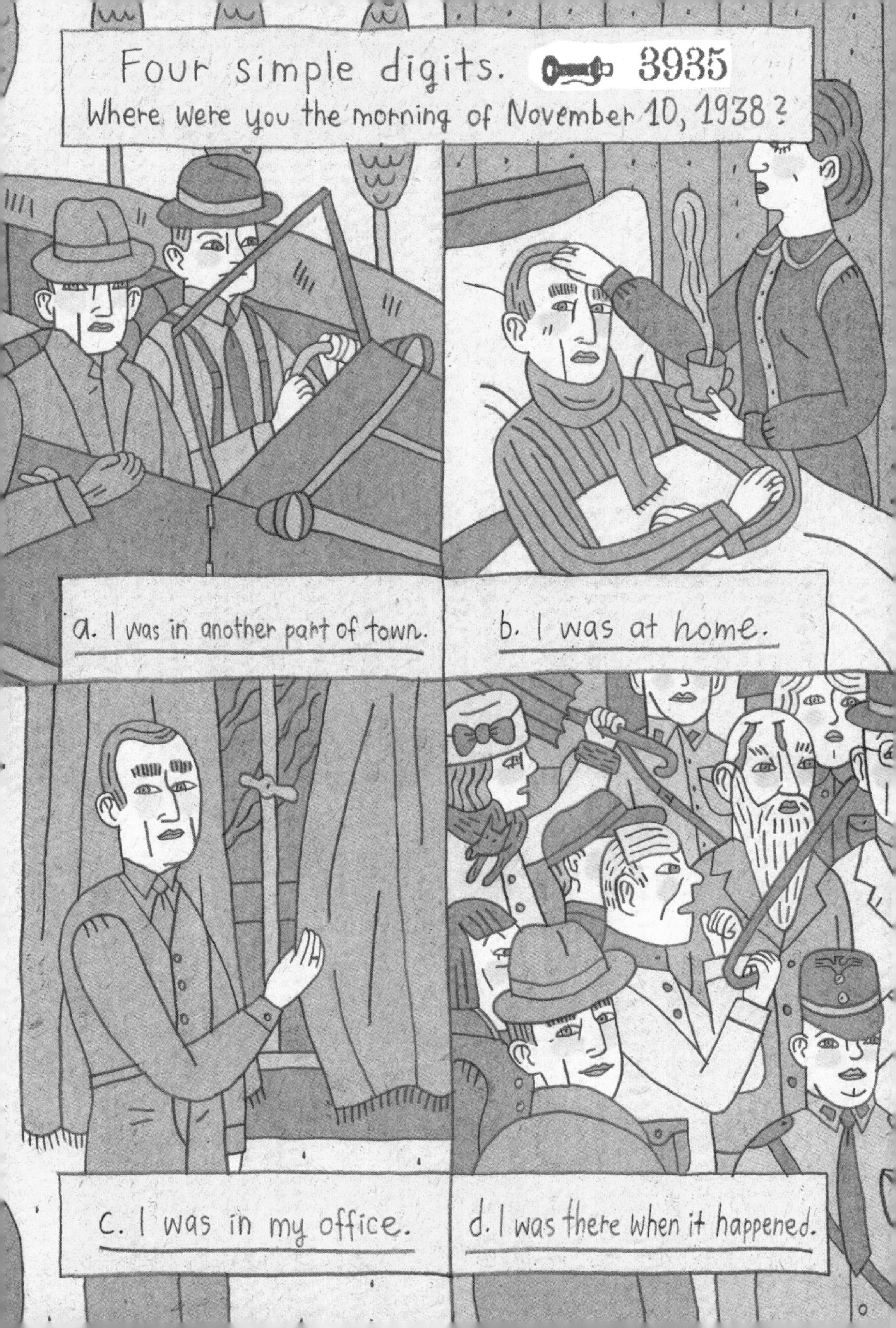

Four simple digits. 3935
Where were you the morning of November 10, 1938?
a. I was in another part of town.
b. I was at home.
c. I was in my office.
d. I was there when it happened.

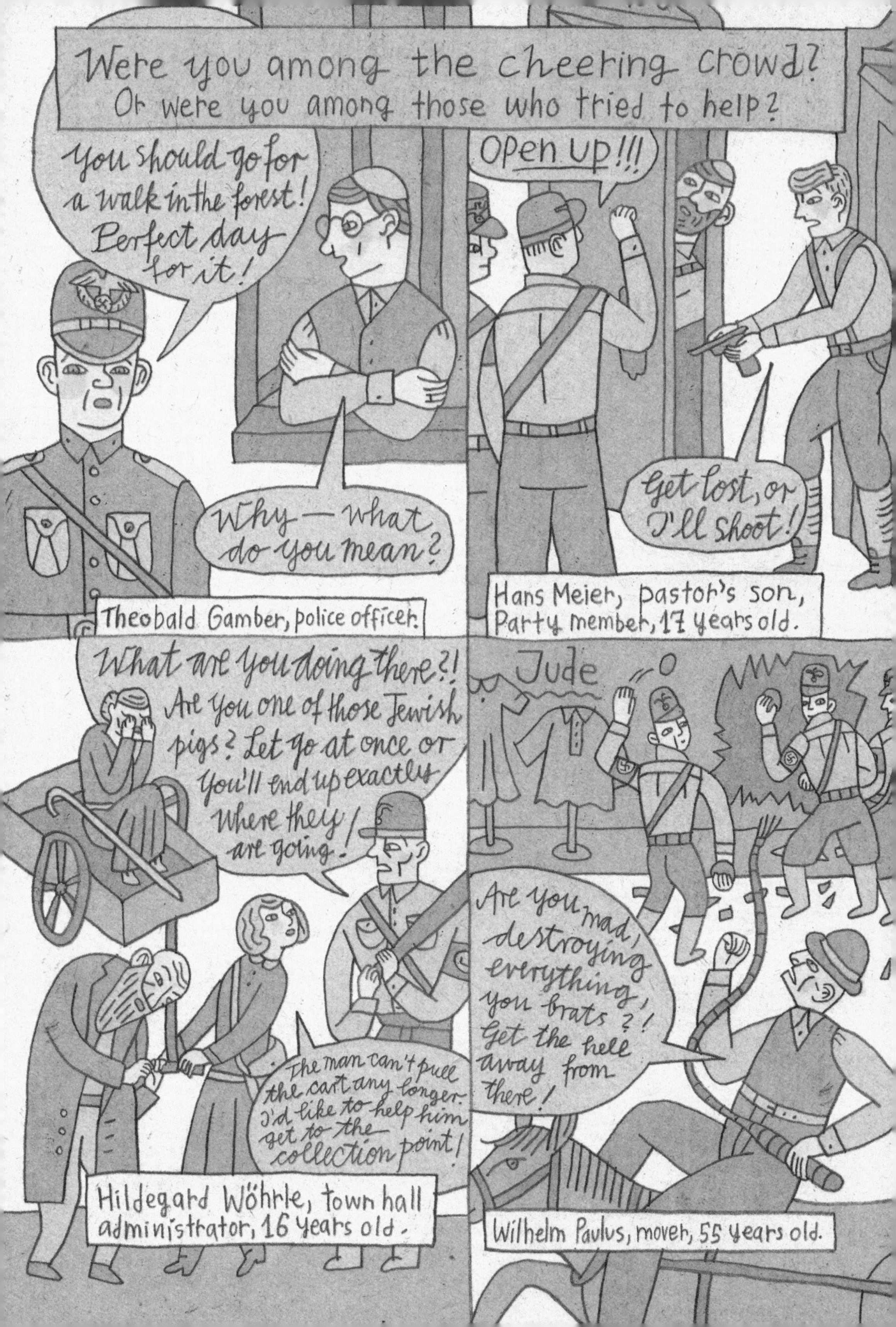
Were you among the cheering crowd?
Or were you among those who tried to help?
You should go for a walk in the forest! Perfect day for it!
Why—what do you mean?
Theobald Gamber, police officer.
Open up!!!
Get lost, or I'll shoot!
Hans Meier, pastor's son, Party member, 17 years old.
What are you doing there?! Are you one of those Jewish pigs? Let go at once or you'll end up exactly where they are going!
The man can't pull the cart any longer. I'd like to help him get to the collection point!
Hildegard Wöhrle, town hall administrator, 16 years old.
Jude
Are you mad, destroying everything, you brats?! Get the hell away from there!
Wilhelm Paulus, mover, 55 years old.

Hundreds of Jews were arrested and taken to Dachau concentration camp that day. The Jewish community was charged a fine and instructed to tear down the burned-out synagogue, now deemed "decrepit" and "dangerous to public safety." A reservoir for extinguishing fires resulting from the Allied bombings was installed, instead.

I pull the 1940 phone book from the shelf.

For the first time, Jewish citizens are listed in a separate category:

---

III. 322                Jüdische Einwohner

# Jüdische Einwohner

---

In August of that same year, Karlsruhe's mayor writes a letter to the local police chief:

"Constant complaints have been made by both the municipal tram staff as well as the public about the fact that local Jews have been behaving brashly and provocatively in crowded tram cars and have refused to give up their seats for German women."

At an address just around the corner from Willi's apartment, I find a Jewish man named Julius Hirsch, a soccer legend who played on the 1912 German Olympic team.

Was Willi a soccer fan? Or was he as oblivious of his Jewish neighbor's existence as I was of the fact that the Hirsch travel agency, where we went to book our family vacations all throughout my youth, was owned by a man who survived Theresienstadt, whose father, a onetime famous soccer player, had lived right around the corner from my grandfather?

Hirsch — Jul. Israel, Murgst. 7.3

Three years after the publication of this phone book, Julius Hirsch will decline an offer by a friend to be smuggled out of Germany in a postal van, and he will be deported and his name erased from the annals of German soccer. Although he will disappear in Auschwitz, his name will hover like a specter in the phone books until 1944.

In 1940, Karlsruhe's Sinti and Roma were deported to Poland. That same year, together with another GAULEITER, Robert Wagner ordered the arrest of over 6,500 Jewish men and women in the region. On October 22, almost one thousand Jews gathered at Karlsruhe's train station. Their destination was a French-run concentration camp in Gurs, in the Pyrenees. From there, many were transferred to Auschwitz a couple of years later.

"The procedure was hardly noticed by the general public," SS general Reinhard Heydrich stated right after the Jews' arrest. Robert Wagner declared Karlsruhe's state the first to be JUDENFREI (Jew-free).

In 1941, the "Jewish Citizens" section disappears from the phone books.

The 1941 phone book lists the names of all those with whom Willi shares an office building. The Catholic Student Union, originally housed on the second floor, but banned by Heinrich Himmler for its "subversiveness" in 1938, has disappeared.

Willi now shares his floor with a Reich Labor Service leader and a field marshal. Emilio Just, specialist of "Foreign Wines and Southern Fruits," owns Weinhaus Just, a wine bar located on the building's ground floor.

On the top left corner of the page is an ad for Weinhaus Just. Is this where Willi stood, in the darkness behind the white curtain, on November 10, 1938?

**Weinhaus Just**
Spezialität: Auslands-Weine und Südfrüchte
Kaiserstraße 91 — Fernruf 4259

Hoping to get closer, I look for artifacts from Weinhaus Just online. There is an autograph for $299 of Franz Hugos, magician extraordinaire, master of clairvoyance, hypnosis, and handkerchief tricks, who performed at Weinhaus Just in 1932, but I decline.

Another item pops up for sale on the screen, and this time I am hooked: a postcard with a 1930 Easter greeting. "Did you not receive my letter? I hope to hear from you soon," writes a lovesick Mr. Albert to a standoffish Miss Medert.

The front of the card features a photograph of the interior of Weinhaus Just.

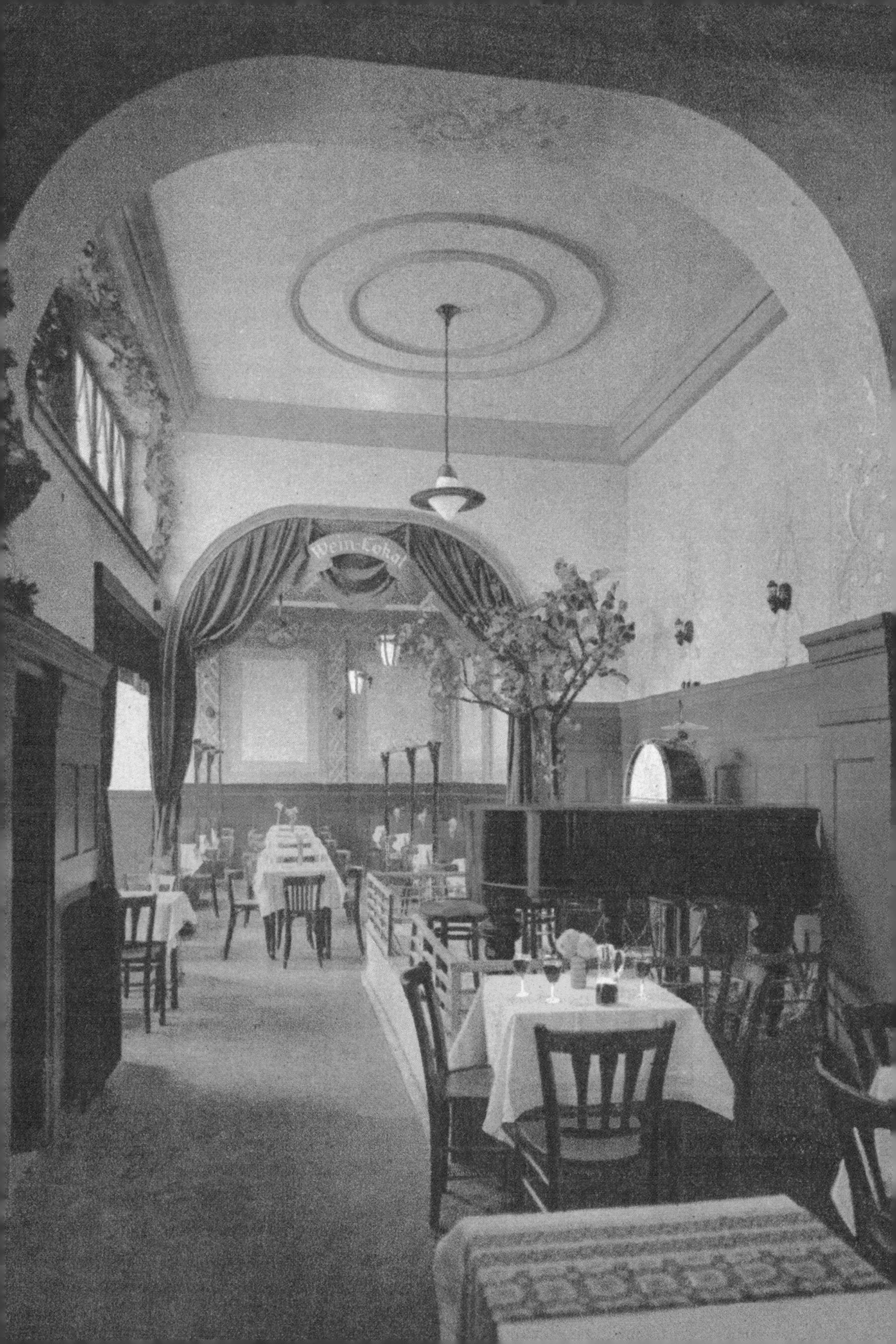
Wein-Lokal

I look at the postcard and I imagine Willi entering the restaurant after a long day at the office. I see him leave his mothball-scented flannel hat with the maître d'. I hear the chair move across the carpeted floor as he pulls it out from under a table to sit down. His fingers smooth out the tablecloth, and he picks up the small vase to smell the pink flowers. In heavy local dialect, he orders a carafe of red. He cranes his neck to catch a glimpse of Franz Hugos behind the grand piano, and when a violin is tuned and a tuxedoed singer walks into the spotlight, I see him tap his foot to the rhythm of the German tango: "You black Gypsy, you know my pain. And when your violin cries, my heart cries the same!"

And all I need to do is sit down on the chair across from him in the midst of the music and the happy tipsiness and look at him and put my hand on his and ask him the questions I've always been burning to ask.

The archivist catapults me out of my daydream: "Your file is waiting for you in the reading room."

# 11.
# SOFT
# RETURN

A few days after my visit to the archive in Bronnbach, my father drops me off at Külsheim's castle square. I've decided to stay here for a few days on my own. I wave goodbye and watch my father drive off toward the road that leads back to Karlsruhe. Then I set foot in the town where his family has lived for generations.

Külsheim i. Baden

Just like thirty years ago, when my brother and I were released into these streets so we could look at Annemarie's house from the outside, I try to tread on the pavement as softly as I can. This is the pavement on which my uncle Franz-Karl once walked; here are the houses he once passed and the fountains he drank from. And here are the grounds of the castle where my father sat and played by himself when he skipped kindergarten; here is where he walked to school on an empty stomach.

I can feel my father's unhappy childhood creep up through the soles of my feet. Here is his old HEIMAT that expelled him and, because of that, allowed him to become who he is now.

I feel a sudden panic — a longing for my father, as if I won't ever see him again.

I have arranged to meet with Egon, a local amateur historian whom I found online, hoping he will shed some light on what it was like to grow up in Külsheim under the Nazi regime, hoping that I can learn through him what I'm not ready to learn from my own family:

Who was my uncle Franz-Karl, whose shadow my father has lived in all his life, whom I've needed to know about since I stood by his grave in Italy, whose absence fractured our family?

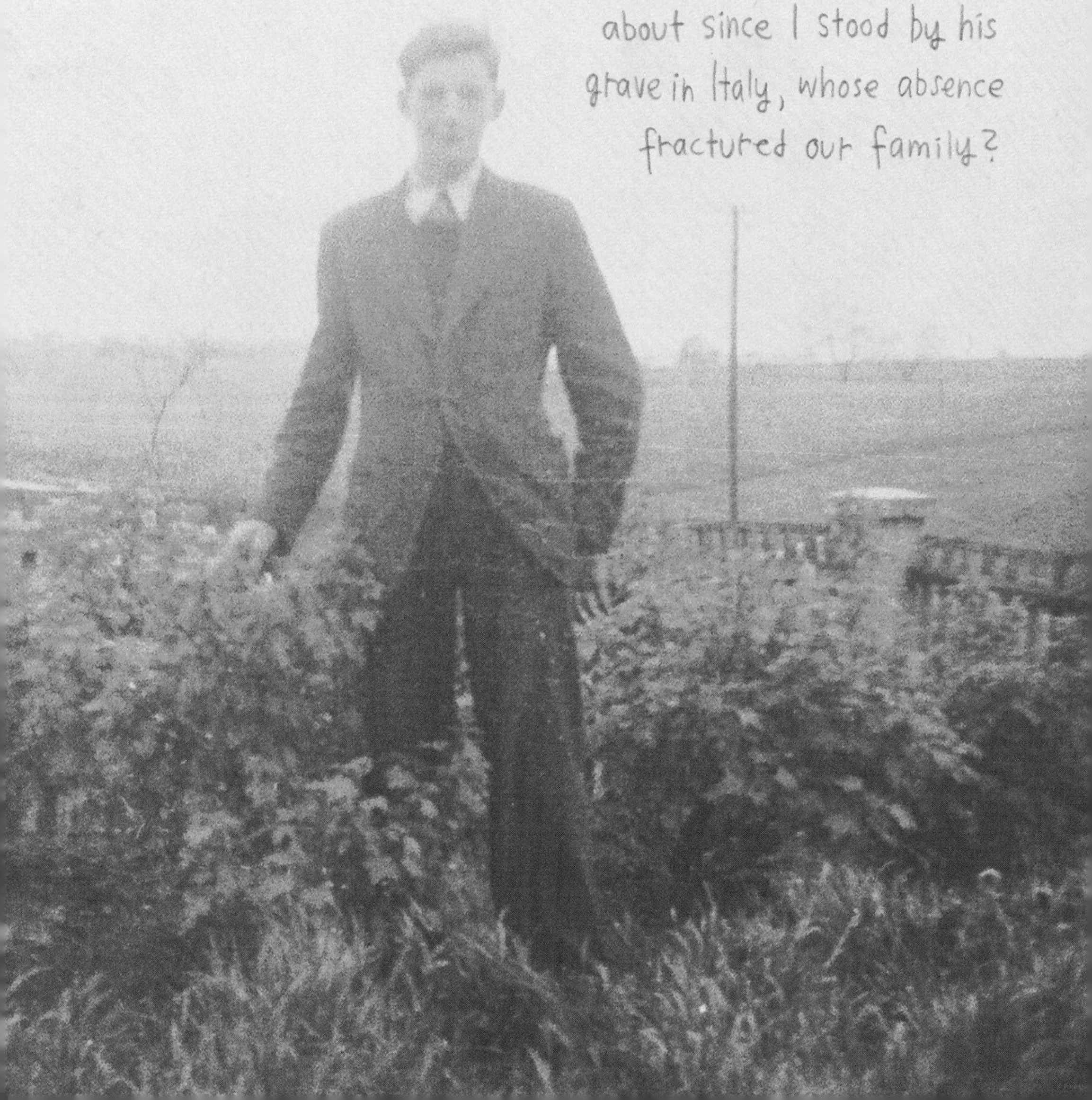

Egon is tall. His straight posture and shock of white hair exude self-confidence. As we walk down Külsheim's main street, he lets me know that "none of the other historians can tell you more than I can."

Perhaps, in a small town such as this, for some, owning the memory of the Jews is synonymous with owning up to one's own guilt.

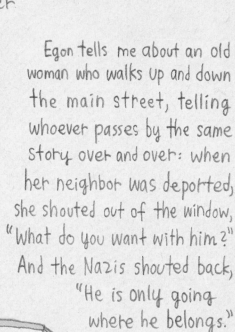

One of Egon's relatives was Külsheim's mayor until 1933. After the Nazis came to power, he hid one of the synagogue's Torah scrolls under his floorboards, to save it from burning.

Egon's father was there when Külsheim's Jews were pushed into the water. "He tried to intervene," Egon says, "but one of the Nazis told him that if he did, he'd end up in the fountain, too."

Egon tells me about an old woman who walks up and down the main street, telling whoever passes by the same story over and over: when her neighbor was deported, she shouted out of the window, "What do you want with him?" And the Nazis shouted back, "He is only going where he belongs."

In 1988, the 50th anniversary of REICHSKRISTALLNACHT, Egon tells me, Külsheim's city council agreed that a memorial plaque should be placed where the synagogue used to be. But because some people in town were concerned that Pater Grimm's (the priest executed for resisting the Nazi regime) memorial site would look insignificant in comparison (and anyway, wouldn't it be better to leave the past behind?), the matter was abandoned.

Egon shows me the empty spot where the synagogue once stood, and the house where the Jews were imprisoned before their deportation. He points out the dent on a house where a mezuzah once hung, and where a Turkish family now lives. He unlocks the door to a dilapidated barn where an old mikvah, a Jewish ritual bath, uncovered under a rotting stack of hay not long ago,

is decaying in between an unhinged door and an old plow. He shows me the headstones of the first (1695) and the last (1938) person ever to be buried in the Jewish cemetery and points out a tombstone whose marble plate is missing.

It was removed during the war, under cover of night, by an unknown person. "Why would anyone do that?" I ask.

Egon says, "There's a rumor that a certain person in town stole it to use it as flooring in a kitchen."

As a parting gift, Egon hands me my family tree — the first I've ever seen — dating back to 1732. "This one fell down the stairs," he says, pointing out a Karl-Joseph Krug, who broke his neck in 1888. Thanks to Külsheim's amateur genealogist, I finally have a narrative to tell: In our family, falling seems to be a common cause of death.

Labels on photo: town hall, fountain, Alois & Maria, M.N.?, hotel

A 1920s photograph shows my grandparents Alois and Maria walking down the main street on their wedding day, past the fountain where the Jewish men were pushed under the water in 1939, and past the hotel where I am staying. In the photo, a man leans out of the window right below where I am standing now. Is it Meier Naumann, the local Torah scribe, who owned the building — a kosher restaurant — back then?

My room is sweltering. It is the hottest month of the year and the hottest time of day. Beyond the rubber tree on my windowsill I can see the deserted town hall square and its medieval fountain. Hot-pink geraniums hang down from it like thirsty tongues. Bearded sandstone faces spout water from their yawning mouths. Right behind the fountain, a crucified Jesus is watching, just as he watched that day in 1939. It says in chiseled letters beneath his bleeding feet, ES IST VOLLBRACHT (It Is Done).

That evening, I meet Hans, another local historian, for a drink.
I'm only a few sips into my Riesling when I realize that the beer garden

where we are sitting in the shade of an old chestnut tree is that
of my great-grandfather's restaurant, still named Rose.

As I look at the façade, I try to imagine my father sitting behind it,
blowing into a spoon full of hot bone-marrow-dumpling soup.

Hans has a soft voice and an open gaze. He talks about the history of Külsheim's Jews with neither sentimentality nor self-righteousness. One day, he tells me, the thousands of pieces of paper, the photographs and recorded interviews he is archiving in his house, will make it into a published book, a compendium of every single thing there is to know about the Jews of Külsheim. When he isn't in his office at the German armed forces, or performing his duties at the local soccer club, or at the carnival society, or traveling to France to celebrate the friendship between the German and the French Former Prisoners of War Associations, Hans loses himself in the archive, or interviews the old people in town over a beer. Around the corner from the Rose an old house is being dismantled, and Hans is distraught that he didn't get there in time to save its old tiles, which were laid there by a Jewish former owner of the house, and which Hans wanted to salvage for his future museum of Külsheim's Jewish history. "I should have inquired about them earlier," he says, and shakes his head.

Hans is obsessed, and I feel that I have found an ally.

When Hans started to interview the people in town in the 1980s, no one seemed to remember anything. Everyone was "working in the fields," "out of town taking driving lessons," or

otherwise busy when someone switched off the town's main fuse one night and the Jews' windows were smashed with stones under cover of darkness; when the Jews were forced to submerge in the water; when the short circuit ripped through the synagogue; and when "the people were loaded onto a lorry and brought to an unknown place." Over time, fragmentary stories, photographs, and documents rose back to the surface like bloated corpses. Memories turned into legends, and sometimes, legends turned into memories.

Not everyone in town appreciates Hans's inquisitiveness. "Be careful," one man warned him years ago, "or you'll be the first to be gone when the Nazis are back!" But as long as he doesn't talk politics, Hans gets along with everyone, he says, even the man who tells his dog that "the Jew put that there" when he doesn't want it to eat a discarded piece of food on the street.

Hans calls Theo, a childhood friend of my aunt Annemarie's, who is in his 80s. Theo joins us at the beer garden for a second round of drinks.

"I was there when the synagogue burned down," Theo says, and takes a sip from his beer.

"There were about a hundred people there, and none of them ever doubted that it was done on purpose."

After the war, the electrician who caused the short circuit at the synagogue founded ELEKTRO-HAUS, an electronics business.

"Was my uncle there when it happened?" I ask.

"I don't remember."

"Did you know my uncle?"

"Yes, of course I did," Theo says.
"He was just a few years older than me."

"What was he like?"

Theo's eyes light up
under his bushy brows.

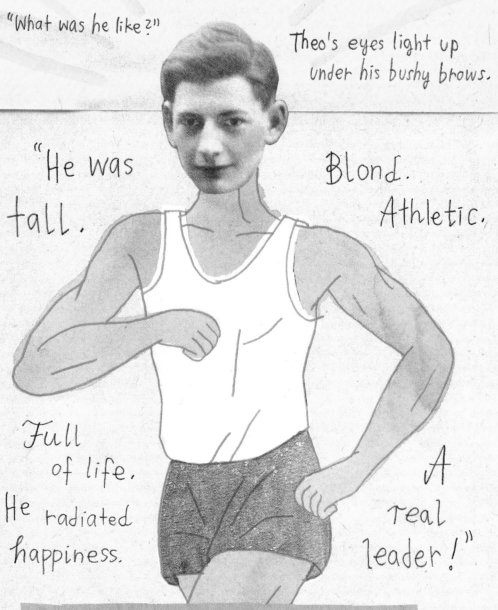

"He was
tall.

Blond.
Athletic.

Full
of life.
He radiated
happiness.

A
real
leader!"

Blond? I wonder. A leader? My uncle?

"I remember when he was recruited," Theo says.

Put "SS" here

NEXT!

"Many were drafted right into the SS and used as cannon fodder.

There was a celebration up on the hill, to see your uncle and the other recruits off. It was a memorable evening."

"Do you know anything about my grandparents' political views?" I ask.

"No. I only know that they were richer than most. They were thought of as modern because they owned a car.

Your aunt Annemarie was modern, too. Unusual for her time. She always wore pants."

Theo looks down at his beer and smiles, as if in admiration of my aunt.

On the way back to my hotel,
I stop in front of a medieval house on the
main street. Its plastered façade is painted
neatly in light pink and red. A shiny sign next
to it informs me that it was recently restored with
the help of the German Landmark Foundation.

Right behind it stands the decrepit barn
with its forgotten old mikvah.

One of ELEKTRO-HAUS's
vans is parked
next to it.

Its engine
starts and I watch
as it disappears toward
Pater Grimm Street,
toward the edge of the town.

Through Hans, I connect with Walda, the widow of my father's cousin. My father hasn't spoken to her in almost 50 years.

Three different home-baked cakes, wine squeezed from the grapes of a nearby vineyard, a row of teddy bears on the back of the sofa: Walda's hospitality takes me hostage. She touches my arm frequently. Even her face looks like a soft pillow. The moment I enter her house, she decides that I am part of the family: "You look like a Geier," she says, referring to my great-grandfather Heinrich, Maria's father. "Dark, slim, and tall." Even without Egon's family tree dating back to the 1700s, my physical connectedness is apparent.

Everybody here, except me, knows where I belong.

Geographically. Historically. Genetically.

In May 1945, Walda was a teenager, and she was terrified. Her father was the mayor, and he was going to be held accountable.

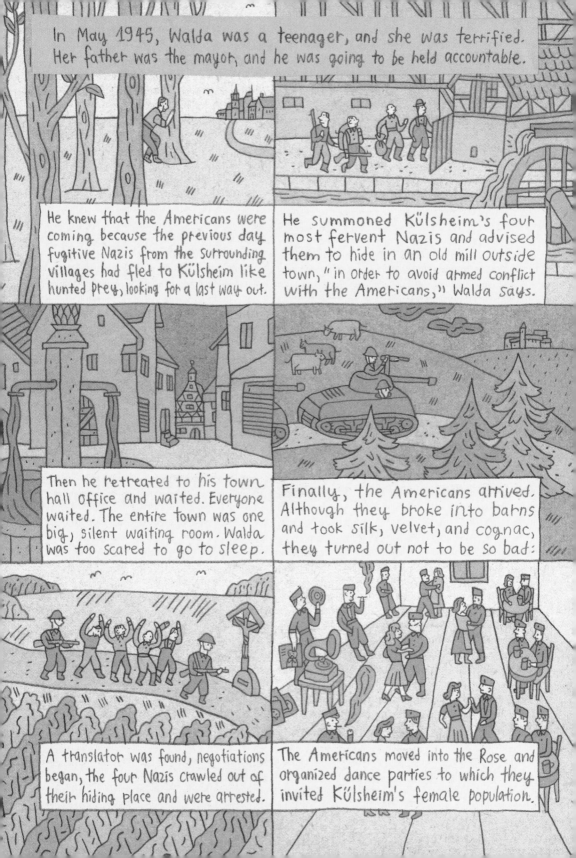

He knew that the Americans were coming because the previous day fugitive Nazis from the surrounding villages had fled to Külsheim like hunted prey, looking for a last way out.

He summoned Külsheim's four most fervent Nazis and advised them to hide in an old mill outside town, "in order to avoid armed conflict with the Americans," Walda says.

Then he retreated to his town hall office and waited. Everyone waited. The entire town was one big, silent waiting room. Walda was too scared to go to sleep.

Finally, the Americans arrived. Although they broke into barns and took silk, velvet, and cognac, they turned out not to be so bad:

A translator was found, negotiations began, the four Nazis crawled out of their hiding place and were arrested.

The Americans moved into the Rose and organized dance parties to which they invited Külsheim's female population.

"She always wore white, to show that she was rich enough to let the farmhands do the for her time. In 1939, Vienna with a group Walda questioningly, makes me conclude a scandalous affair at least. "Annemarie from school for a her from the Alois's death, plum schnapps ment, Maria the man who in her back- to leave account father. unusually to your

work. She was unusual she disappeared to of soldiers." I look at and her quiet smile that Maria had with one of them, had to be removed while, to protect shame. After while distilling in the base- told me that dyed uniforms yard wanted his savings to your He was kind father."

Walda gives me
a meaningful look.

"You mean Alois wasn't
my grandfather?"

"I don't know." Walda smiles.

"Your father didn't have it easy. I can still see him as a boy, standing in front of my house, asking for something to eat.

It still hurts my soul when I think of it."

Later, when I tell my father about all the things that Walda said, I can tell by the way he looks at me in silence that he is deeply moved. "I don't know anything about a savings account," he finally says.

My great-grandfather Franz-Karl's initials — FKK, the initials he shared both with my uncle and my father — still adorn the entrance to the 300-year-old farmhouse next to Walda's house, where he once lived. Its attic is a family vault, and I have come to see if any of my uncle Franz-Karl's things are hidden here.

100-year-old dusty flour sacks bearing my family's name lie piled up in an old chest. A certificate made out to my great-grandfather for winning a silver medal at a 1906 Farming and Gardening Fair leans against a wall in a broken frame. A cardboard box holds drawings by his grandchildren from 1936 and 1937: mouse-eaten dreams of hunting poisonous-mushroom-grown forests for game.

I can find neither my uncle Franz-Karl nor the answers to my greater questions here. After accidentally turning dozens of spider families out of their homes, I leave the dust to settle for more decades to come.

# 12.
# FOLLOWING
# THE FLOCK

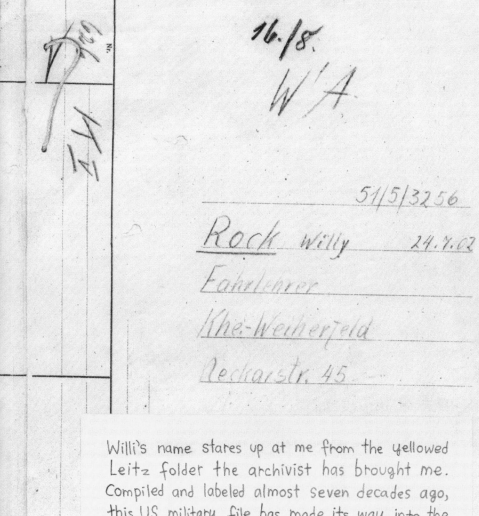

51/5/3256

Rock Willy    24.7.02

Fahrlehrer

Khe-Weiherfeld

Neckarstr. 45

Willi's name stares up at me from the yellowed
Leitz folder the archivist has brought me.
Compiled and labeled almost seven decades ago,
this US military file has made its way into the
daylight — for the first time in two generations.

I sit down and peel back its cover.

# MILITARY GOVERNMENT OF GERMANY

## Fragebogen

**WARNING:** Read the entire Fragebogen carefully before you start to fill it out. The English language will prevail if discrepancies exist between it and the German translation. Answers must be typewriter or printed clearly in block letters. Every question must be answered precisely and conscientiously and no space is to be left blank. If a question is to be answered by either "yes" or "no", print the word "yes" or "no" in the appropriate space. If the question is inapplicable, so indicate by some appropriate word or phrase such as "none" or "not applicable". Add supplementary sheets if there is not enough space in the questionnaire. Omissions or false or incomplete statements are offenses against Military Government and will result in prosecution and punishment.

**WARNUNG:** Vor Beantwortung ist der gesamte Fragebogen sorgfältig durchzulesen. In Zweifelsfällen ist die englische Fassung maßgebend. Die Antworten müssen mit der Schreibmaschine oder in klaren Blockbuchstaben geschrieben werden. Jede Frage ist genau und gewissenhaft zu beantworten und keine Frage darf unbeantwortet gelassen werden. Das Wort „ja" oder „nein" ist an der jeweilig vorgesehenen Stelle unbedingt einzusetzen. Falls die Frage durch „Ja" oder „Nein" nicht zu beantworten ist, so ist eine entsprechende Antwort, wie z. B. „keine" oder „nicht betreffend" zu geben. In Ermangelung von ausreichendem Platz in dem Fragebogen können Bogen angeheftet werden. Auslassungen sowie falsche oder unvollständige Angaben stellen Vergehen gegen die Verordnungen der Militärregierung dar und werden dementsprechend geahndet.

## A. PERSONAL / A. Persönliche Angaben

1. List position for which you are under consideration (include agency or firm). — 2. Name (Surname). (Fore Names). — 3. Other names which you have used or by which you have been known. — 4. Date of birth. — 5. Place of birth. — 6. Height. — 7. Weight. — 8. Color of hair. — 9. Color of eyes. — 10. Scars, marks or deformities. — 11. Present address (City, street and house number). — 12. Permanent residence (City, street and house number). — 13. Identity card type and Number. — 14. Wehrpass No. — 15. Passport No. — 16. Citizenship. — 17. If a naturalized citizen, give date and place of naturalization. — 18. List any titles of nobility ever held by you or your wife or by the parents or grandparents of either of you. — 19. Religion. — 20. With what church are you affiliated? — 21. Have you ever severed your connection with any church, officially or unofficially? — 22. If so, give particulars and reason. — 23. What religious preference did you give in the census of 1939? — 24. List any crimes of which you have been convicted, giving dates, locations and nature of the crimes.

1. Für Sie in Frage kommende Stellung: **Fahrlehrer**
2. Name **Rock**   **Willy**   3. Andere von Ihnen benutzte Namen
   Zu-(Familien-)name    Vor-(Tauf-)name
   oder solche, unter welchen Sie bekannt sind. **keine**
4. Geburtsdatum **24.7.02**   5. Geburtsort **Karlsruhe**
6. Größe **1,78m**   7. Gewicht **69 Kg.**   8. Haarfarbe **d.blond**   9. Farbe der Augen **grau**
10. Narben, Geburtsmale oder Entstellungen **keine**
11. Gegenwärtige Anschrift **Karlsruhe, Neckarstr. 45**

12. Ständiger Wohnsitz

13. Art der Ausweiskart...    ... **keine**
16. Staatsangehörigkeit    ...nd Einbürgerungsort an.

18. Aufzählung aller Ihr...    ...ine

19. Religion **evang.**
Verbindung mit einer Kir...    ...t betreffend

23. Welche Religionsangehörigkeit haben Sie bei der Volkszählung 1939 angegeben? **evang.**   24. Führen Sie alle Vergehen, Übertretungen oder Verbrechen an, für welche Sie je verurteilt worden sind, mit Angaben des Datums, des Orts und der Art. **nicht betreffend**

### B. Grundschul- und höhere Bildung

| Name & Type of school or military Name und Art der besonderen NS oder Militärakademie geben Sie dies an | Ort | Wann besucht? | Certificate Diploma or Degree Zeugnis, Diplom oder akademischer Grad | Did Abitur permit University matriculation? Berechtigt Abitur oder Reifezeugnis zur Universitätsimmatrikulation? | Date Datum |
|---|---|---|---|---|---|
| Volksschule | Karlsruhe | 1909-1917 | Abg.Zeugnis | nicht betr. | nicht be... |

25. List any German University Student Corps to which you have ever belonged. — 26. List (giving location and dates) any Napola, Adolph Hitler School, Nazi Leaders College or military academy in which you have ever been a teacher. — 27. Have your children ever attended any of such schools? Which ones, where and when? — 28. List (giving location and dates) any school in which you have ever been a Vertrauenslehrer (formerly Jugendwalter).

25. Welchen deutschen Universitäts-Studentenburschenschaften haben Sie je angehört? **keinen**
26. In welchen Napola, Adolf-Hitler-, NS-Führerschulen oder Militärakademien waren Sie Lehrer? Anzugeben mit genauer Orts- und Zeitbestimmung. **keinen**
27. Haben Ihre Kinder eine der obengenannten Schulen besucht? **nein**   Welche, wo und wann? **nicht betreffend**

28. Führen Sie (mit Orts- und Zeitbestimmung) alle Schulen an, in welchen Sie je Vertrauenslehrer (vormalig Jugendwalter) waren. **nicht betreffend**

### C. PROFESSIONAL OR TRADE EXAMINATIONS / C. Berufs- oder Handwerksprüfungen

| Name of Examination Name der Prüfung | Place Taken Ort | Result Resultat | Date Datum |
|---|---|---|---|
| Gesellenprüfung Fahrlehrerprüfung | Karlsruhe | Prüfg.bestanden | 31. 3. 1920 März 1930 |

*[Handwritten annotations overlaid on form:]*

This is the original form, the exact piece of paper my grandfather once held in his hands.

Finally, Willi is talking to me.

The form lists 313 questions.

Willi fills in the answers with his typewriter on January 10, 1946.

40. Indicate on the following chart whether or not you were a member of and any offices you have held in the organizations listed below. Use lines 96 to 98 to specify any other associations, society, fraternity, union, syndicate, chamber, institute, group, corporation, club or other organization of any kind, whether social, political, professional, educational, cultural, industrial, commercial or honorary, with which you have ever been connected or associated. — Column 1: Insert either "yes" or "no" on each line to indicate whether or not you have ever been a member of the organization listed. If you were a candidate, disregard the columns and write in the word "candidate" followed by the date of your application for membership. — Column 2: Insert date on which you joined. — Column 3: Insert date your membership ceased if you are no longer a member. Insert the word "Date" if you are still a member. — Column 4: Insert your membership number in the organization. — Column 5: Insert the highest office, rank or other post of authority which you have held at any time. If you have never held office, rank or post of authority, insert the word "none" in Columns 5 and 6. — Column 6: Insert date of your appointment to the office, rank or post of authority listed in Column 5.

40. In der folgenden Liste ist anzuführen, ob Sie Mitglied einer der angeführten Organisationen waren und welche Aemter Sie darin bekleideten. Andere Gesellschaften, Handelsgesellschaften, Burschenschaften, Verbindungen, Gewerkschaften, Genossenschaften, Kammern, Institute, Gruppen, Körperschaften, Vereine, Verbände, Klubs, Logen oder andere Organisationen beliebiger Art, seien sie gesellschaftlicher, politischer, beruflicher, sportlicher, bildender, kultureller, industrieller, kommerzieller oder ehrenamtlicher Art, mit welchen Sie je in Verbindung standen oder welchen Sie angeschlossen waren, sind auf Zeile 96—98 anzugeben.

1. Spalte: „Ja" oder „Nein" sind hier einzusetzen zwecks Angabe ihrer jemaligen Mitgliedschaft in der angeführten Organisation. Falls Sie Anwärter auf Mitgliedschaft oder unterstützendes Mitglied oder im „Opferring" waren, ist, unter Nichtberücksichtigung der Spalten, das Wort „Anwärter" oder „unterstützendes Mitglied" oder „Opferring" sowie das Datum Ihrer Anmeldung oder die Dauer Ihrer Mitgliedschaft als unterstützendes Mitglied oder im Opferring einzusetzen.

2. Spalte: Eintrittsdatum.

3. Spalte: Austrittsdatum, falls nicht mehr Mitglied, anderenfalls ist das Wort „gegenwärtig" einzusetzen.

4. Spalte: Mitgliedsnummer.

5. Spalte: Höchstes Amt, höchster Rang oder eine anderweitig einflußreiche von Ihnen bekleidete Stellung. Nichtzutreffendenfalls ist das Wort „keine" in Spalte 5 und 6 einzusetzen.

6. Spalte: Antrittsdatum für Amt, Rang oder einflußreiche Stellung laut Spalte 5.

| | 1<br>Yes or no<br>ja oder nein | 2<br>From<br>von | 3<br>To<br>bis | 4<br>Number<br>Nummer | 5<br>Highest Office or rank held<br>Höchstes Amt oder höchster Rang | 6<br>Date Appointed<br>Antrittsdatum |
|---|---|---|---|---|---|---|
| 41. NSDAP  Nazi Party | ja | 1933 | 1.8. 1940 | 2565949 | keine      none | keine |
| 42. Allgemeine SS | nein | | | | | |
| 43. Waffen-SS | nein | | | | | |
| 44. Sicherheitsdienst der SS | nein | | | | | |
| 45. SA | nein | | | | | |
| 46. HJ einschl. BDM | nein | | | | | |
| 47. NSDStB | nein | | | | | |
| 48. NSDoB | nein | | | | | |
| 49. NS-Frauenschaft | nein | | | | | |
| 50. NSKK | nein | | | | | |
| 51. NSFK | nein | | | | | |
| 52. Reichsb. der deutschen Beamten | nein | | | | | |
| 53. DAF | nein | | | | | |
| 54. KdF | nein | | | | | |
| 55. NSV | nein | | | | | |
| 56. NS Reichsbund deutscher Schwestern | nein | | | | | |
| 57. NSKOV | nein | | | | | |
| 58. NS Bund Deutscher Technik | nein | | | | | |
| 59. NS Aerztebund | nein | | | | | |
| 60. NS Lehrerbund | nein | | | | | |
| 61. NS Rechtswahrerbund | nein | | | | | |
| 62. Deutsches Frauenwerk | nein | | | | | |
| 63. Reichsbund deutsche Familie | nein | | | | | |
| 64. NS Reichsbund für Leibesübungen | nein | | | | | |
| 65. NS Altherrenbund | nein | | | | | |
| 66. Deutsche Studentenschaft | nein | | | | | |
| 67. Deutscher Gemeindetag | nein | | | | | |
| 68. NS Reichskriegerbund | nein | | | | | |
| 69. Reichsdozentenschaft | nein | | | | | |
| 70. Reichskulturkammer | nein | | | | | |
| 71. Reichsschrifttumskammer | nein | | | | | |
| 72. Reichspressekammer | nein | | | | | |
| 73. Reichsrundfunkkammer | nein | | | | | |
| 74. Reichstheaterkammer | nein | | | | | |
| 75. Reichsmusikkammer | nein | | | | | |
| 76. Reichskammer der bildenden Künste | nein | | | | | |
| 77. Reichsfilmkammer | nein | | | | | |
| 78. Amerika-Institut | nein | | | | | |
| 79. Deutsche Akademie München | nein | | | | | |
| 80. Deutsches Auslandsinstitut | nein | | | | | |

84. Deutsche Jägerschaft **nein**

85. Deutsches Rotes Kreuz **nein**

86. Ibero-Amerikanisches Institut **nein**

87. Institut ...
   Juden...

88. Kame...

89. Osteu...

90. Reichsarbeitsdienst (RAD) ...

91. Reichskolonialbund **nein**

92. Reichsluftschutzbund **nein**

93. Staatsakademie für Rassen- und Gesundheitspflege **nein**

94. Volksbund für das Deutschtum im Ausland (VDA)

95. Werberat der deutschen Wirtscha...

Others (Specify) andere:

96.

97.

98.

The revelation envelops me like a burning rash.

99. Have you ever sworn an oa... ...d give particulars. — 101. Have you any relatives who have held offic... ...95 above? — 102. If so, give particular names and addresses, their relati... ...With the exception of minor contributions to the Winterhilfe and ... ...ey or property which you have made, directly or indirectly, to the NS... ...utions made by any natural or juridical person or legal entity thro... ...ipient of any titles, ranks, medals, testimonials or other honors fro... ...honor the date conferred, and the reason and occasion for its besto... ...If so, which one? — 108. For what political party did you vote in t... ...ver been a member of any anti-Nazi underground party or grou... ...er been a member of any trade union or professional or business... ...er been dismissed from the civil service, the teaching profe... ...ance to the Nazis or their ideology? — 115. Have you ev... ...actice your trade or profession been imposed on you for... 116. If you have answered yes to any of the questions fro... ...confirm the truth of your statements.

99. Sind Sie jemals zu einem ... ...a, geben Sie die Organisation und Einzelheiten an

101. Haben Sie irgendwelche V... ...der von Nr. 41 bis 95 angeführten Organisationen haben? **nein** ...Ihrer Verwandschaft sowie eine Beschreibung der Stellung und Organisat...

103. Mit Ausnahme von kleineren Beiträg... ...gen, geben Sie nachfolgend im Einzelnen alle von Ihnen direkt oder indirekt an die NS... ...rganisationen geleisteten Beiträge in Form von Geld oder Besitz an, einschließlich aller auf ... ...einer natürlichen oder juristischen Person oder einer anderen rechtlichen Einheit geleisteten Bei...

104. Sind Ihnen von einer der oben angeführten Organisationen ... ...tel, Orden, Zeugnisse, Dienstgrade verliehen oder andere Ehren erwiesen worden? **nein** 105. Falls ja, geben Sie an, was Ihnen verliehen wurde, das Datum, den Grund und Anlaß für die Verleihung.

**nicht betreffend**

106. Waren Si... ...he politische Partei haben Si... ...aren Sie seit 1933 Mitglied ... ...? n.bet.

113. Wären S... ...chaftsverban- des? **ne**... ...Stellung auf

Grund aktiven ... ...Wurden Sie jemals aus rass... ...t genommen oder in Ihrer B...

116. Ist die Ant... ...on'en, welche dies wahrheitsg...

Seven decades ago, a moist **ja** seeped into this thirsty paper. I trace it slowly with my finger.

My mother and aunt had been wrong.
15% of all Germans joined the Nazi Party,
and my grandfather was among them.

40. Indicate on the following chart whether or not you were a member of the organizations listed below.

| | | | |
|---|---|---|---|
| SS (general) | 42. | Allgemeine ⚡⚡ | nein |
| SS (armed wing) | 43. | Waffen-⚡⚡ | nein |
| SS (intelligence agency) | 44. | Sicherheitsdienst der ⚡⚡ | nein |
| Assault Division | 45. | SA | nein |
| National Socialist Motor Corps | 50. | NSKK | nein |
| Institute for Study of the Jewish Question | 87. | Institut zur Erforschung der Judenfrage | nein |

— 104. Have you ever been the recipient of any titles, ranks, medals, testimonials or other honors from any of the above organizations? —

nein

106. Were you a member of a political party before 1933?  nein

— 108. For what political party did you vote in the election of November 1932?

S.P.D. (Social Democrats) — 109. In March 1933?  S.P.D.

— 114. Have you ever been dismissed from the civil service, the teaching profession or ecclesiastical positions or any other employment for active or passive resistance to the Nazis or their ideology?  nein

— 121. Have you or any immediate members of your family ever acquired property which had been seized from others for political, religious or racial reasons or expropriated from others in the course of occupation of foreign countries or in furtherance of the settling of Germans or Volksdeutsche in countries occupied by Germany?  nein

— 123. Have you ever acted as an administrator or trustee of Jewish property in furtherance of Aryanization decrees or ordinances?

nein

# Meldebogen

auf Grund des Gesetzes zur Befreiung von
Nationalsozialismus und Militarismus vom 5. 3. 1946

Next in the file is a list of 14 questions. Willi answers them in neat handwriting in blue ink on April 23, 1946, and delivers the form to the local police station two days later.

a) _____ IN KARLSRUHE _____ von ____ bis ____

b) _____ von ____ bis ____

Every question must be answered! Based on article 65 of the Law for the Liberation from National Socialism and Militarism, wrong or misleading or incomplete answers will be punished with prison or fines.

- Allg. SS
- Waffen-SS
- Gestapo
- SD. der SS (Sicherheitsdienst)
- Geheime Feldpolizei
- SA. ......... nein
- NSKK. (NS-Kraftfahr-)
- NSFK. (NS-Flieger-Ko...)
- NSF. (NS-Frauenschaft,

4. Were you ever privileged because of your membership in a Nazi organization? nein

5. Did you ever give money to the Nazi Party or another Nazi organization? nein

6. Affiliation with the Wehrmacht, any police group, the Reich Labor Service, Organization Todt, Transport Brigade Speer, etc.?
WEHRMACHT  Highest rank achieved: UFFZ. (officer)  From when: 1.8.1943

Did you act as a leading Nazi officer (including unofficially)? nein

Did you act as a General Staff Officer? nein

11. Have you been or are you currently being tried? Ja
Where? KARLSRUHE  With which result? unbekannt (unknown)

13. How would you rank yourself based under the current law?

MITLÄUFER

Major Offender – Offender – Lesser Offender – Follower – Exonerated Person.

Out of the five options presented to him,
Willi chooses to categorize himself as a Follower.

# MITLÄÜFER

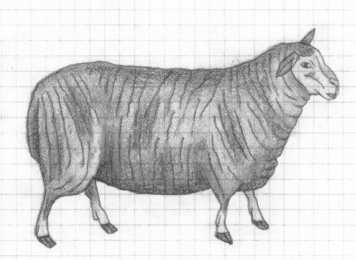

MITLÄÜFER describes a person lacking courage and moral stance.

I imagine Willi sitting at his oak desk with the green-and-orange stamp moistener. The intimacy of seeing the word with which he confesses to his own weak-mindedness, written out in his own handwriting, is hard to bear.

23. APRIL 1946                Unterschrift:        ROCK    Willi
Datum                                      Name        Vorname

Rock        Willi

A Social Democrat and a member of the Nazi Party.
Neither a resistance fighter nor a major offender.

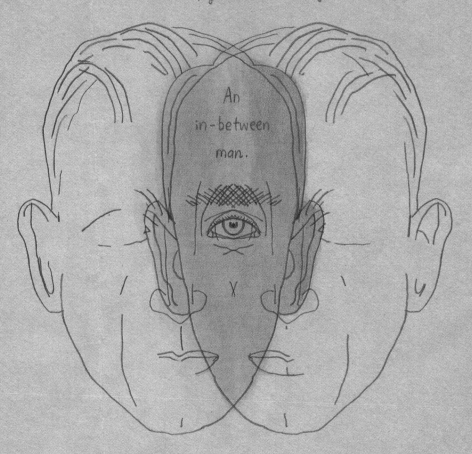

An
in-between
man.

Why did Willi join the Nazi Party only months
after voting for the Social Democrats?
In April 1933, the Nazis froze membership
admissions to discourage opportunists from applying.
Was an exception made for my grandfather?

I turn the page, and in a letter to Karlsruhe's mayor, translated
into English for the occupying forces, Willi answers all my questions:

Willi   R o c k                    Karlsruhe, January 22nd, 1946
Karlsruhe
Neckarstr. 45


The Honorable Ot Mayor ermeister
Karlsruhe.
-----------

Re:  Procedure on Appeals, law no. 8.

        On September 28th, 1945 I handed in a request at the Police
Directory Karlsruhe, in regards to the reopening of a driving school
this request was forwarded to the Wir Economic Affairs Office , Karlsruhe,
for decision. I was then informed thru the Wir Economic Affairs Office
that the permission was dependent on the decision of the Procedure
on Appeals.
        On foundation of section 4 of the regulations under law no
8, I here-by hand in the proposition to introduce the Procedure on
Appeals. To unburden myself, I state the following:
        In the year 1932 I entered into the service of the firm
Dahlhofer and Hummel, Karlsruhe; and in the year 1933, I took over
the business. As the car of the former Rei Reich Governor s Robert
Wagner was in one of the auto - boxes in the garage, the acquisition
of the business was made dependent on my entrance into the N. Nazi Party
Under the pressure of the preceding conditions I joined the party
thru the force used upon me. During my membership I had no office,
rank or other post, nor did I wear the uniform. The money to found
the driving-school was obtained from my wife who had a milk shop for
several years.
        In examining my Procedure on Appeals I kindly ask you to
consider my former relations in regards to the party.
            Inclosed you will find my Frage questionnaire

                    Respectfully yours,

                        Willy Rock

The above statement is verified by:
                        Dranys Lengenbacher. Heinzinger

As witness in regards to my statement that I was organized untill
1933, in the free union, I refer to Altstadt Council Member loesser
Karlsruhe, Gottesauerstr. 45, who was manager of the " Gesamtver-
bandes  Federation of Employees of Public Business and Trade d des Personen
Warenverkehrs. "

Robert Wagner —

the man who endorsed the burning of the synagogue, who sanctioned the sterilization and killing of those "unworthy of life," imprisoned "anti-social elements," Communists, Social Democrats, and the "politically subversive," ordered the strangulation of the Jewish lawyer Ludwig Marum, deported hundreds of Sinti and Roma and thousands of Jews

— parked his car in the garage of the driving school my grandfather intended to buy.

Willi Rock                                        Kalrsruhe, den 22. Januar 1946

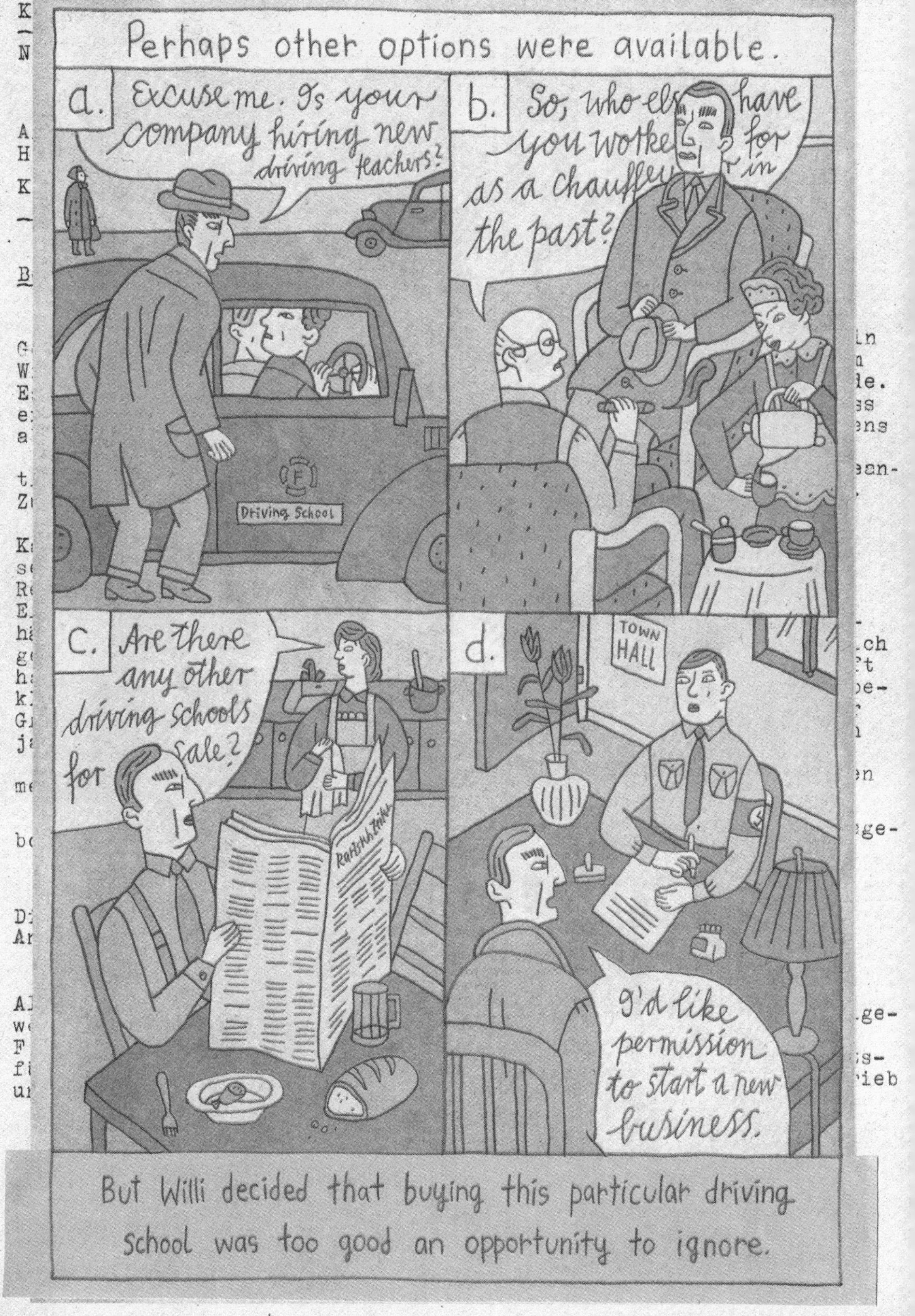
Perhaps other options were available.
a.
Excuse me. Is your company hiring new driving teachers?
Driving School
b.
So, who el… have you worke… for as a chauffe… in the past?
c.
Are there any other driving schools for sale?
d.
TOWN HALL
I'd like permission to start a new business.
But Willi decided that buying this particular driving school was too good an opportunity to ignore.

Did the money for the driving school really come from Anna's milk shop?

Or is Willi just afraid of facing repercussions if he mentions that the money had instead been given to him by a Jew?

If the money did come from the milk shop, then what had the Jewish employer's money really been for? Some part of me would like to believe that it was given to him in exchange for a hiding place in an inconspicuous shed.

# Things German | №6 | das Brot

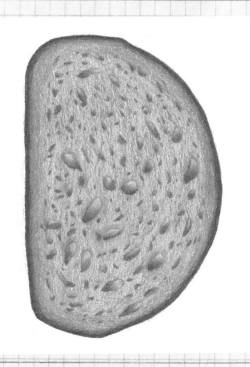

The first thing I do when I get off the plane in Germany is look for the nearest bakery. The perfect bread is big and heavy — dark, hard, and crusty on the outside, and glutinous and sour on the inside. Its smell reminds me of the forest. When I ask Germans living abroad what they miss about their home country, many name SCHWARZBROT (dark bread) as most important.

According to the Central Union of the German Baking Trade, over 3,000 bread recipes are registered in Germany. Germany has recently applied for its bread to be recognized by UNESCO as an object of Intangible Cultural Heritage. The traditional evening meal, a selection of sliced breads with cheese or sausage, is called ABENDBROT (evening bread). BROTZEIT (bread time) is the Bavarian term for "snack." FREIHEIT UND BROT (freedom and bread) was a popular Nazi Party slogan. After the war, the radical Jewish group Nakam (Revenge), whose aim was to avenge the victims of the Holocaust by killing 6 million Germans, smuggled arsenic into a bread factory in Nuremberg and brushed 3,000 loaves, destined for former members of the SS held in prison camps, with the poison. Two thousand prisoners were poisoned, but none died.

At the time Willi writes his letter to the mayor,
Karlsruhe still lies in ruins.

531,000 fire and phosphorous bombs, 22,000 tons of demolition bombs,
and 420 aerial mines left tens of thousands in the city homeless,
thousands injured, and hundreds dead.

A year earlier, the French liberated Alsace,
crossed the Rhine, which borders Karlsruhe, and fought
their way into the city.

The head of police and the chief of the JUDENAMT
(Jew Bureau) ▓▓▓▓▓▓▓▓▓▓▓▓▓ committed
suicide.

The police went on a desperate all-night drinking binge.

There was heavy street fighting, but soon,
white flags appeared in the windows.

Buildings on Adolf ▓▓▓▓▓▓▓▓▓ Hitler Square
were evacuated and set on fire by the French to be
used as a dramatic backdrop on French newsreels.

Department stores, slaughterhouses, and wine cellars
were looted by the Germans and the French.

Women were raped,
their babies later aborted.

Tens of thousands arrived from Germany's former Eastern territories, displaced and in search of food and shelter.

Jews emerged from garden sheds.

Concentration camp survivors were picked up by bus and, for lack of a change of clothes, walked the streets in their striped uniforms.

Some were met with flowers and tears, others with resentment for being allocated additional food stamps.

Notorious Nazis were taken to denazification camps.

Robert Wagner's wife and daughter were paraded through the streets of Strasbourg. According to one account, Wagner's wife was abducted into an Algerian brothel in Paris, where she took her own life. Robert Wagner turned himself in and was executed.

Then, the Allies decided that Karlsruhe should be ruled by the Americans. The French moved out, and the American flag was hoisted in Karlsruhe's main squares.

his work permit has been frozen, his office has been bombed, and his car has been stolen by a French soldier.

He seeks employment as a day laborer, and his salary amounts to a tenth of what he had previously earned.

Food is scarce. On the narrow strip of grass behind their house, Anna grows vegetables and keeps a chicken for eggs.

She travels to the countryside to exchange her dowry for potatoes and sells the coffee Elsa sent from Switzerland on the black market.

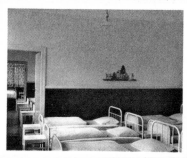

The Red Cross diagnoses Karin with malnourishment and sends her to a sanitarium in Switzerland, where French and German children are fattened up with cod-liver oil. Letters home are written in pencil and censored by the staff. German children are separated from the rest of the group during mealtimes and forced to eat everything on their plates — including any food they fail to keep down.

## 13

Willi Rock
Faarscaullearer

Karlsrume Raein

==========================================

Neckarstrasse 4;

Karlsrume, den lo.9.46

*Meldebogen* Nᵒ *3256*

On September 10, 1946, Willi writes a letter to the public prosecutor:

bei der Spruchkammer  Karlsrume
Oberpostdirektion

Attached to this letter I am submitting four testimonials in my defense which prove that I was forced to enter the party in 1933 because of the conditions at the time, that I was in no way engaged in National Socialist activities and always vocalized my disregard for the party, and that the party and its organization didn't interest me in any way.

...

My wife was dispossessed of her milk business on July 1, 1939, because she neither joined the party, nor the National Socialist Women's League. My wife had taken over the business from her parents, who ran it for 21 years prior to that.

...

I haven't been able to work as a driving teacher ever since my dismissal from the German Armed Forces in April 1945. I therefore ask for a decision at your earliest convenience, so that I can carry out my profession and support my family (wife and two children). I should be regarded as a mere MITLÄUFER, and I hope to be classified into that category.

TWO CHILDREN. I feel a pang in my chest.
At the time the letter is written, my mother is four months old.
Suddenly, I feel more lenient toward Willi.

For a brief moment, I give in to the illusion that, perhaps, my grandmother's political integrity can make up for the lack of Willi's.

I walk over to the phone books and open the 1940 volume under M. I find the category for **Milch** (milk) and scan the column for the letter R: Anna's name stares up at me defiantly. **Rock Anna, Haßingerst. 7** Her shop is still in business in 1940. Uneasily, I pull out the 1941 volume, and there it is again, still located at the same address **Rock Anna**, and it returns again in 1942, this time written in Antiqua font (because FRAKTUR-SCHRIFT has been declared un-German, allegedly a font invented by Jews at the dawn of printing) **Rock Anna**, and it remains there all through 1944, until it finally vanishes in the slender 1945/46 edition.

Is Willi lying about the dispossession of the milk business? Or is Anna's name just a hovering ghost, like the one of Julius Hirsch that lingered on in the phone books even after his death in Auschwitz?

# Things German | N° 7 | die Gallseife

GALLSEIFE, popular in Germany since the mid-1800s, is a soap made of ox gallbladder. It is biodegradable and perfume-free. The gallbladder's natural salts work against the most persistent stains, especially when applied with a WURZELBÜRSTE, a scrubbing brush made out of wood and vegetable fibers. Many Germans living in the United States complain about the shortness of American wash cycles (45 minutes vs. 2.4 hours), low water temperatures (120 Fahrenheit vs. 194 Fahrenheit), and, as a result, the excessive use of bleach. Stains on white fabric deeply unsettle me. Even on the "whitest whites" setting, my American washing machine doesn't bring back a fabric's original purity, and I rely on GALLSEIFE and Persil, a time-tested German laundry detergent invented in 1907. Some referred to the postwar testimonials written by neighbors, colleagues, and friends in defense of suspected Nazi sympathizers as PERSIL CERTIFICATES. Persil guarantees your shirts to come out as white as snow.

Next in Willi's file are five testimonials affirming his innocence. The letters sound flat and formulaic.

Walter S., architect

"Based on my own experience, I can confirm that Mr. Willi Rock... never held an office within the Nazi Party and never engaged in any activities on behalf of the party. He never wore the party emblem and always spoke against the party's doings."
August 20, 1946

"I've known Mr. Willi Rock for over 20 years. ... I got to know Mr. Rock as a colleague of decency and good character, who lived only for his business and his family. ... Rock never wore the party emblem and never acted like a party member."
September 3, 1946

Otto H., driving teacher

Emilio J., owner of Weinhaus Just

"I attest herewith that Willi Rock, ...whose office was located in my building..., never acted like a Nazi. ... Furthermore, I can confirm that I didn't even know that Mr. Willi Rock was a party member because I never saw him in uniform, nor saw him wear the party emblem. ..."
August 28, 1946

If what Emilio writes is true, then why did Willi pose
in uniform in some of his photographs?
Because he wanted to commemorate a moment in history?

Because he wanted to be
remembered as a patriot,
if he didn't return from Belgium?

Because Anna thought that
a uniform would look more
impressive in the family album?

Or was it just to be part of a romantic tradition?

The next witness, a mechanic named Erich W.,

provides a copy of his letter in English.

Karlsruhe, January 10th, 1946

The Honorable OberMayormeister of Karlsruhe.

Re: Procedure on Appeals under Law no. 8,
conducted thru Mr. Willy Rock,
Karlsruhe, Neckarstr. 45.

As avowed "Antifaschist" I can assure that Mr. Willy Rock, with whom I am acquainted for many years, was according to his remarks never a convinced Nationalsocialist. It was due only to the former conditions and pressure that Mr. Rock became a member of the Nazi Party.

Thru frequent intercourse with Mr. Rock I had the impression that he condemned the methods of the Nationalsocialists, they were abhorrent to him. Mr. Rock was never a participant in any political offences.

I can assure that this sentence is made with the best of knowledge in regards to Mr. Rock.

Respectfully,

The German Union of Antifascists' website fills me in on the details of Erich W.'s life and I feel momentarily relieved:

Whose testimonial can be trusted if not that of a member of the Communist resistance, arrested by the Nazis in 1933, charged with high treason and sent to a concentration camp, chained to a radiator and beaten with a snap hook and the leg of a chair?

Erich was released by the Nazis in 1936.

The 1942 phone book lists him as living on the same street as my grandparents.

How dangerous was it to befriend a known Communist in 1942? Would Willi have befriended a concentration camp survivor if he had truly believed in the Nazis' ideology?

Hochachtungsvoll

Karlsruhe, 30. August 1946.
Karl Wilhelmstr. 1b.

It is the last of the five letters, written by a merchant

E r k l ä r u n g !
========

named Albert W., that convinces me most.

Mit Herrn  W i l l y  R o c k,  Karlsruhe-Weiherfeld Neckar=
strasse

I've been acquainted with Mr. Willy Rock ... since 1926.
We were both employed by the Kahn Brothers company.
... Even after we left the company in 1929/1930, we saw
each other very often, until Mr. Rock was drafted into
the military in 1940. ... Mr. Rock, who ... was a Social
Democrat in his young years, entered the party in 1933
under pressure of the conditions at the time. ... When the
Nuremberg Laws came into effect in 1935, Mr. Rock
explained to me that he would have never joined the party
if he had known about the party's goals beforehand,
and that he would strictly refuse to join additional
organizations from then on. ... His inner conviction
prevented him from joining any activist organization
that required its members to wear a uniform. Even
though Mr. Rock knew that I am married to a Jewish
woman, and even though relations with people in mixed
marriages were critically eyed, Mr. Rock stood by us
always and at any time. I am willing to vouch
anytime and under oath that Mr. Rock was never
an activist and never engaged in any Nazi activities.

As if to convince me, the person assessing the letter underlines
the letter's most important arguments in red:
"His inner conviction prevented him";
"I am married to a Jewish woman."

Albert vouches for my grandfather's innocence,
unconditionally, "anytime and under oath" —
the very thing I have always been unable to do.

I feel Albert's words in the pit of my stomach.
Something unlocks there, in the silent darkness.
A radiating warmth. Hot-water-bottle warmth.
A tenderness toward my grandfather.

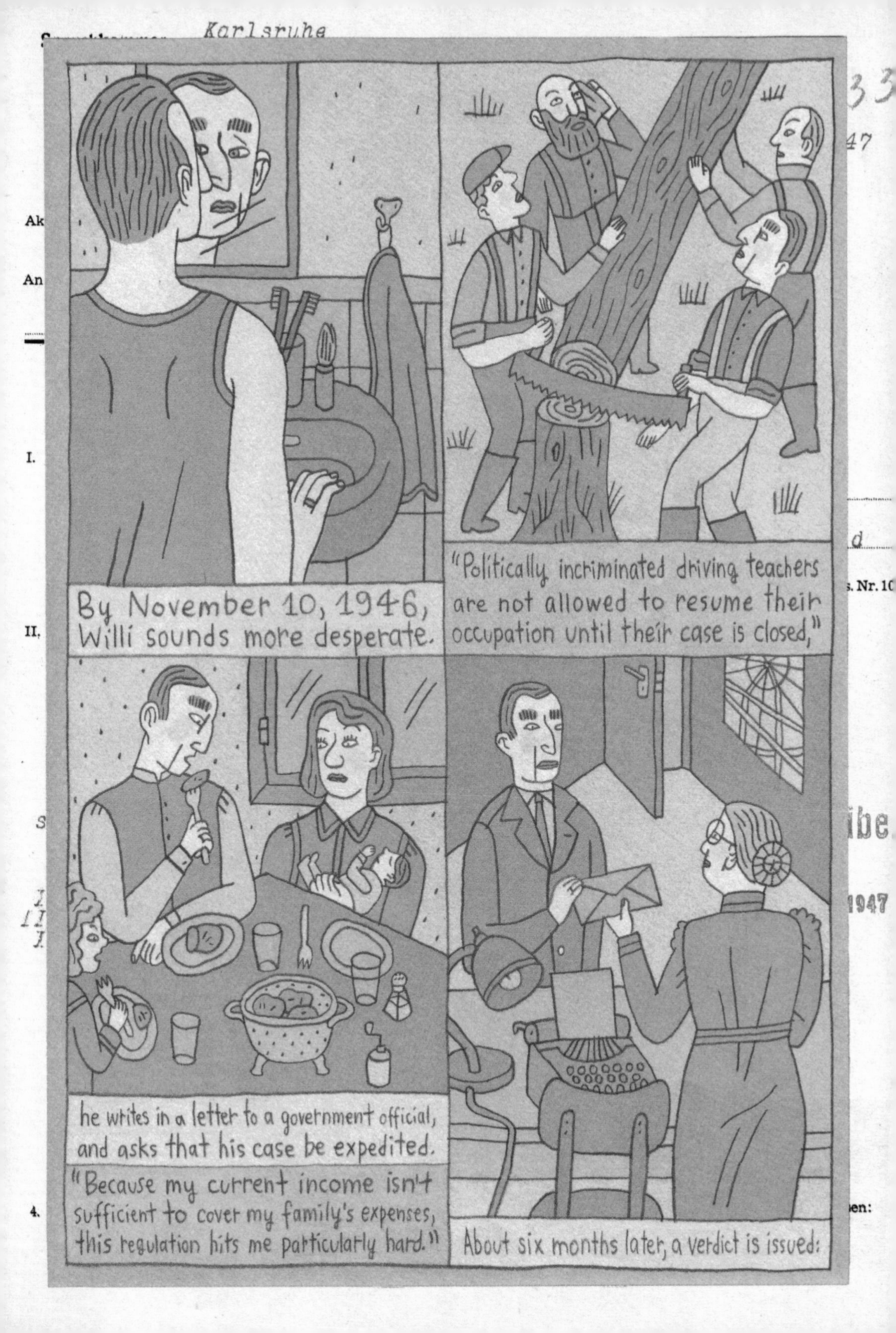
By November 10, 1946, Willi sounds more desperate.
"Politically incriminated driving teachers are not allowed to resume their occupation until their case is closed,"
he writes in a letter to a government official, and asks that his case be expedited.
"Because my current income isn't sufficient to cover my family's expenses, this regulation hits me particularly hard."
About six months later, a verdict is issued:

"A lawsuit is brought against driving teacher _Willy Rock_. Rock was a member of the Nazi Party between 1933 and 1945. He was also a member of the National Socialist People's Welfare organization. ... A move is made to designate the person concerned as an OFFENDER."

Suddenly, I find myself on Willi's side.

Maybe he had lied on the questionnaire about quitting the party in 1940 and about not having joined the National Socialist People's Welfare organization, and maybe even about Anna's milk business.

And yet, I feel my heart sink as I read the word OFFENDER.

Spruchkammer V Karlsruhe                          Den 11. Juli 1947

Aktenzeichen: 51/5/3256 - O.Z.: S-626

# Spruch

On May 3, 1947, Willi writes a last letter to the public prosecutor, pleading to be downgraded into the group of FOLLOWERS. A final verdict is issued three months later and sent to the public prosecutor, the police department, the employment bureau, the military government, and the Ministry for Political Liberation:

gegen                                                              r. 45.

im sch

der
halb                                                         hat. L
Anle                                                         il A de
Arti                                                         gen des
in d                                                         e an si
Zif.                                                         und § 2
einz                                                         Verfahr
Die                                                          g vom
4.4.

According to the law, the person concerned falls into the group of OFFENDERS because he joined the Nazi Party before May 1, 1937. He certifies by submitting testimonials that he joined the party under pressure, that he was never actively engaged in any Nazi activities, and that he always spoke against the party. ... Additional testimonials confirm that he refused all attempts to convince him to join the National Socialist Motor Corps, even though joining would have been self-evident in his professional position. ... It is thus concluded that the person concerned never put into practice any of the offenses under article 7-9. ... Because all other requirements under article 12 I of the law are met, the person concerned should be ranked as a FOLLOWER. Due to the Christmas Amnesty Regulation of February 5, 1947, the lawsuit has been suspended.

Der Spruch- ... ...scheic-
ist rechtskräftig seit 16.8.47
25 AUG 1947
Karlsruhe, den

The final verdict comes as a relief to me.
I try to imagine the relief Willi must have felt.
I also wonder what it was like to live with the knowledge that you
had once been labeled a FOLLOWER — a person lacking courage
and moral stance, an animal that follows the flock.

I have reached the end of the file.

I close the cover and stare at the table. My head feels heavy
with the echo of Willi's voice, with the voices of his friends
and the voices of those who directed the course of his life,
heavy with my own voice. I feel drained by all the conversations
I had with him, and with myself, over the past few hours, and
still unsure about their meaning.

I lift my head and emerge from the depths of my grandfather's
life. As I make it to the surface, I fill my lungs with air.

My mother waits for me in the car outside Karlsruhe's archive. "How was it?" she asks, as I sit down in the passenger's seat.

She is picking me up so we can go for an ice cream at one of the cafés established by the Italian GUEST WORKERS who came to help rebuild the country in the 1950s.

"Willi was in the Nazi Party," I reply with the detached confidence of a schoolgirl who delivers a well-researched essay to her history teacher.

"Really?!" She stares at the moving road ahead. "I never would have thought that."

She lowers her window to let the shock evaporate.

"Well, I don't think he was a bad person," she finally says. "But I always thought he was a bit of a coward."

A few days later, my aunt Karin takes me for a ride. We drive by my grandfather's old apartment and the building where Anna's milk business was once located.

"You have to put yourself in Willi's place," Karin says. "He had to support a family. What would you do if you were told you'd lose your job unless you joined a particular party?"

"It was the Jews and the 'politically unreliable' who lost their jobs, not the eighty-five percent who didn't join the party," I say, trying to sound calm.

"Think about it. With no radio, how would he have even known what Hitler's politics were all about?"

By 1941, 65% of all households owned either Joseph Goebbels's PEOPLE'S RECEIVER,

the Nazis' most important propaganda tool, or some other type of transmitter.

"Do you know for sure that he didn't own a radio?" I ask.
"No... I don't." Her voice sounds softer.

I don't blame her. Everyone has just one father.

# 13.
## PEELING
## WALLPAPER

I'm on my way to one of Külsheim's neighboring towns, to meet my cousin Michael, my father's nephew, for the first time in my life. The small talk I engage in with my cabdriver,

about the unusually hot weather and Külsheim's annual wine festival, fails to keep my nervousness at bay.

I cling to a small bottle of plum schnapps I've brought as a gift, decanted from my grandmother Maria's demijohn that's kept in my parents' basement.

Maybe it's the animals —
the horses that stand still as
Michael and I gaze at the
surrounding vineyards; the
cockatoo that stares at us
from its cage in the bathroom,
as Michael gives me a tour of his
veterinary clinic; the cats that look on from a safe
distance behind the bushes as his wife walks me
around the garden;
the turtles that feign
ignorance from under
the surface of the
pond as I engage in a
first, timid conversation
with Michael's daughters; the dogs
that nudge us with their wet noses as
we carry our food from the grill to the
patio table — that makes meeting
my cousin and his family feel less
difficult than I had imagined.

Over sausages, potato salad, and Maria's (by
now unbearably strong) plum schnapps, we
catch up on decades of missed conversation.
We talk about "big Franz-Karl," as they call my uncle here,
and "little Franz-Karl," as they call my
father. And we talk about Annemarie,
who never mentions the war nor big
or little Franz-Karl,
Michael's wife says.

Michael grew up knowing little about my father, only what Annemarie had told him: that he was a university professor and owned a villa in France — in reality a tiny, insufficiently renovated farmhouse equally rich in charm and in mildew.

"I think big Franz-Karl's death has something to do with why my mother holds a grudge against your father," Michael says.

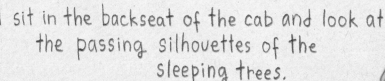

"We told her that you're here," his wife adds. "Maybe we can get her to agree to meet you, too, next time you visit."

Darkness has descended on the deserted vineyards and forests by the time I leave my cousin's house. It is the kind of darkness that makes you become invisible, even to yourself.

I sit in the backseat of the cab and look at the passing silhouettes of the sleeping trees.

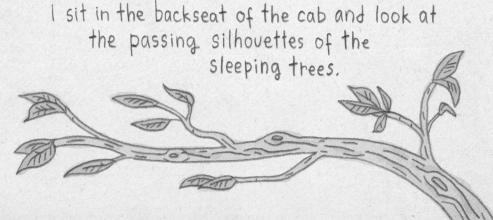

I open the window and let the darkness in.
What does it take to reconstruct a fractured family?

The air is filled with the chirping of crickets.
Its fragrant dampness makes me feel secure.

The next day I call Michael's sister, Iris — the cousin whom my brother and I had seen in the doorway of Annemarie's house some 30 years ago — but she doesn't recognize my name. Nervously, I tell her who I am and that I'd like to meet.

Iris lives in my great-grandparents' farmhouse, right next door to Annemarie. The sudden proximity to my aunt unsettles me. But when I pass by the stables and cross the courtyard, when I enter the house and walk up the same stairs with the painted pattern of green leaves that my father and my uncle Franz-Karl walked up every day, I begin to feel more comfortable.

And when I enter the kitchen and see the homemade cakes on the table, I realize that Iris is as excited to meet as I am. "There is a rumor that our grandfather Alois went to prison because he spoke out against the Nazis," Iris tells me, "but I don't know if it's true."

She gives me a tour of the old farmhouse and points out three cut-out, painted wooden figures hanging on the wall, of characters in Disney's BAMBI. "Big Franz-Karl made them for Annemarie," says Iris. Tokens of love from the dead brother, memorializing him forever.

Iris shows me a photograph of Mr. Steinert, the teacher whose red pen marks I had examined in my uncle Franz-Karl's exercise books, and who had marked his essays with "St." I stare at Mr. Steinert, who looks so different from the stout, whiskered man I had imagined standing in my uncle's classroom.

The picture shows him on an outing with his son and Annemarie.

He is wearing a WEHRMACHT belt, and a copy of the local Nazi paper, VOLKSGEMEINSCHAFT, is lying on the grass in front of him.

Even though my uncle isn't in the picture, I feel his presence. Judging by my aunt's age, he would have been about twelve years old at the time the picture was taken — the age he was when he wrote the story about the poisonous mushroom, almost the age I was when I first discovered his illustrated exercise books. For a moment, I feel my uncle's childhood merge with mine.

Mr. Steinert lived next door, Iris tells me. He was drafted into the war and never returned. When the war was over, his wife threw his golden Nazi insignia into the outhouse pit.

Iris's husband and Michael's family join us for coffee and after the first piece of cake, I ask if we can visit the attic, where my father's bedroom used to be. Up in the attic, standing in my father's room, I remember the stories he told me about his childhood. I feel a sudden pain, shallow but sharp and all-consuming as a paper cut, because even inherited memory hurts.

The room was converted into a storage space long ago. Crusty paint buckets and glass jars stand forgotten in the middle of the floor. A piece of marble, and a dusty mirror, clouded from years of neglect, rest against the wall. The only things that still recall the existence of my father are the half-open, empty cupboard in the corner, the dirt-covered sink on the wall, and the room's faded, peeling wallpaper: in reassuring repetition, Bambi and his rabbit friends run off into the distance, past a gentle-looking owl and a lonely stag, and a group of mushrooms, on and on, toward the peeling forest they will never reach.

Iris's husband suggests I take a piece of the wallpaper to show to my father.

Michael's youngest daughter pulls off one of the peeling pieces and hands it to me.

Standing here,
I feel like a half-empty
room with infinite
layers of wallpaper,
each one exposing
what was there before.

My father doesn't remember the wallpaper. But he recognizes the wooden figures in the photographs I took of them and he immediately recognizes the signature on their backs: "This is my signature! These weren't made by my brother. They were made by me!"

And he is right: BAMBI was released in 1942, one year after the Nazis had banned Walt Disney's movies. The white-tailed deer didn't make it into German theaters until 1950. By that time my uncle was already dead.

All these years, Annemarie's family had thought of my father's wooden figures as tokens of love from the dead brother. Tokens affirming the presence of big Franz-Karl, and erasing that of his little brother.

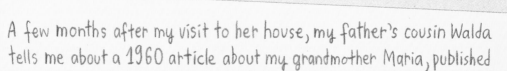

A few months after my visit to her house, my father's cousin Walda tells me about a 1960 article about my grandmother Maria, published in the East German magazine NEUE BERLINER ILLUSTRIERTE. I find a copy on eBay. Because Maria had joined the BUND DER DEUTSCHEN, a West German pro-Communist party opposing West Germany's rearmament, and was running for state representative on its slate, the magazine chose her as the subject for its story "Pleading and Praying Is Futile."

# Bitten und beten zwecklos

**Bittere Erkenntnis für 80 württembergische Bauern**

"At the edge of the Oden Forest, there lies Külsheim. For months, all hell has been breaking loose in this town. A mandate of the federal defense ministry threatens to rob 1,500 acres of farmland from peasants here. ... Now they protest. ... They ask their government: Why do you forcibly rob us of our fertile farmland, when you claim that your aim is to create peace and freedom? ..."

"Farmer Marie Krug took us to the sports field where barracks will be built and pointed at the forest that will be felled to make space for military exercises. She herself will be robbed of ten acres of land. 'Then I'll be practically ruined,' she told us. ...Farmer Krug, whose farm is one of the oldest in Külsheim, is desperate. Her situation is similar to those of thousands of others in West Germany."

**Räummaschinen auf fr barem Bauernland**

Frühling 1960 in Westdeuts Kein Pflug, sondern Räumma rattern über den Acker und b den Aufbau der Offiziersvillen v Bäuerin Marie Krug zeigte u Kanalisation; führte uns zum platz, der für den Bau von K vorgesehen ist; wies auf den der für das Übungsgelände werden soll. Ihr selbst will Bo Hektar Land rauben. Sie sag „Dann bin ich praktisch r Ihren einst 45 Hektar großen mußte sie nach dem tödlichen ihres Mannes schon auf 13 reduzieren. Vorläufig soll sie je noch neun behalten. Nutzlos auf ihrem einst großen Hof d lungen und Scheunen. Sie sir Bäuerin Krug, deren Hof in K mit zu den ältesten gehört, zweifelt. Ihr Beispiel steht in sende ähnlicher Fälle in Westa land. *Text: U. Gebhardt, Fotos: H.*

Golden glänzt der alte Opferstock in der Sonne. Heute stellen die Bauern keine mehr auf. Gegen Gewalt hilft doch kein Beten.

Bitter sind die Tränen der Marie Krug. Im letzten Krieg hat sie ihren Sohn verloren. Jetzt soll sie nun nach und nach um den Rest ihres ererbten, einst reichen Hofes gebracht werden.

"Marie Krug's tears are bitter. She lost her son in the last war. Now, bit by bit, she will be cheated out of her remaining inheritance that was once a prosperous farm."

## Ob im Odenwald, in Hessen oder im Westerwald

überall trifft man auf Spuren der Aufrüstung, auf Beispiele der friedensfeindlichen Bonner Politik. Solche Schilder, wie unter dem Wegweiser nach Stein (links oben), sind auf den kahlen Höhen des Westerwaldes keine Seltenheiten. Viel Land liegt hier schon brach. Ackerboden, auf dem für den Krieg exerziert werden soll. Die Bauern von Stein (rechts) erwarten täglich die Vertreter der Flurbereinigungskommission. Aber sie wollen ihr Land nicht auch noch hergeben, wollen sich wehren. So wie es die hessischen Bauern in Haßloch taten. In ihren Wäldern sollten Raketenabschußbasen stationiert werden. Gemeinsam mit ihrem Pfarrer, Heinrich Grisshammer aus Hitzkirchen (links unten), traten sie öffentlich immer wieder für eine „friedfertige Politik" gegen den „Untergang durch Aufrüstung" ein. Pfarrer Grisshammer ist entschlossen, gemeinsam mit den Bauern und Bürgern von Haßloch nicht nachzugeben, so lange den Kampf zu führen, bis die Atomgefahr endgültig gebannt ist.

Shortly after the article was published, a local newspaper responded with its own West German anti-Communist propaganda. The article is all lies, it says. Mrs. Krug will receive a hefty sum for each of the fields she will lose. What's being built on Mrs. Krug's property aren't barracks, but new houses for the people in town. "Marie Krug's 'tears' are bitter," the article says, "very bitter, indeed, not because injustice is being done to her, but because she represents a cause that stops at nothing, that lies audaciously, and that has no right to claim to be representative of anyone who lives in the liberated West. ... All we can say is 'congratulations to the BUND DER DEUTSCHEN for this candidate.'"

Everyone in Külsheim read the article in the local newspaper, except my father, who was away at boarding school when it was published. Around the same time, Annemarie wrote the letter I had found at Külsheim's archive: "After all it's not our fault that my brother, who was a farmer and would have cultivated the land today, died in the last World War."

"How does it make you feel, reading this article?" I ask my father. "Oh well. I'm not particularly moved. And I don't think my mother really was pro-Communist. I think she just wanted to be someone special."

Liana-like weeds have crawled their way up the dogwood tree.
New rosebush branches shoot sky-high, now riddled with fungus.
Brown corpses of strawberries lie rotting in the grass. My cats have
spotted me and come running, hurdling over the fences that divide us.
They cry and purr and circle my legs to tell me that their bowls are
almost empty. What do they know about war and history and guilt?

Creating order in my domestic chaos promises simple satisfaction. But while I
tear down the weeds, cut back the boxwood, prune the roses, while I pick
up the diseased leaves, my mind is preoccupied with Willi, with my uncle
Franz-karl, and with all the people I spoke to while I was away.
I've excavated the shards of my relatives' existence, but I don't know yet how
to piece them back together.

# 14.
# BLINDING
# WHITENESS

Fall passes quickly.

Women wearing feathers and glittery bikinis pass by my house in Brooklyn during the West Indian Day Parade.

We celebrate Rosh Hashanah with my husband's family, where his nephew sings in Hebrew and we eat the challah he made.

We roast a Thanksgiving turkey and help ourselves to thirds.

It's getting colder, and I build outdoor shelters for the stray cats.

A few weeks later, I call my mother. She has received a copy of Willi's military file. Her nose sounds stuffy, and I know that it isn't from a cold.

"I never really considered that he had suffered, too," she says, and blows her nose. "Reading about his Nazi Party membership wasn't easy. I did wonder why he thought that it was really necessary to join the party. He was no hero. But I'm still convinced that he never did anything really horrible. I was relieved when I read the letter that the husband of the Jewish woman wrote for him. I felt unburdened by it in a way."

The weariness with which she usually talks about her father is gone. Perhaps Willi's file allows her for the first time to look at him for who he was. Not as the person she knew growing up — a father trapped in a repressed, prudish postwar middle-class society — but as a man who had experienced the war, someone who had had to fight to make ends meet to allow her to live and to become who she is now. The woman who had me and made me who I am.

She blows her nose again and she doesn't know that I am crying, too.

Winter has arrived and I can't get Albert W. off my mind — the man whose letter had unconditionally vouched for Willi's innocence, "anytime and under oath," the letter that had meant to exonerate my grandfather from the guilt that I have been carrying around with me for all these years.
I feel an urge to connect with him.

I turn to Google to find out more.
Several Albert W.'s live in the United States, but only one whose name is paired with a Selma. But then, Google wilts my hope: two obituaries inform me that both Albert and Selma died in 1988, the same year as Willi. I am too late again.
What if they had children?
Would they have known their parents' friends?

Google produces two men by the same last name as Albert's: Walter W., who is registered as living in the same town in New Jersey where Albert and Selma had lived and who is listed with an additional address in Florida, and Albert W. III, who lives in a neighboring New Jersey town.

I draft a letter to each of them, include my email address, and put them in the mail.

A couple of days later, a message from Albert W. III arrives in my in-box: his family is Catholic, he writes, they stem from a long line of lumberjacks and emigrated from the forests of southern Germany to the United States in 1763. This is not the man I'm looking for.

Greetings from

_____

FLORIDA, THE LAND OF SUNSHINE

There is still no response from Florida.

Public records show that the house listed under Walter W.'s Florida address was bought in 1999. If Walter is retired and a snowbird, then chances are good that he is in his 70s or 80s now. If his mother and father were born around the same time as Willi, and if they had a child in their twenties or early thirties, mathematically speaking this could be the son of my grandfather's friend.

I look up Walter W.'s Florida address on Google Street View and take a virtual drive down his road. Lawns are shorn to crew-cut length. Perfectly maintained houses are painted in pastel colors.

Walter's house is painted bright blue.
A solitary palm tree stands proud and disheveled in the front.
Green shrubbery sprouts from the banks of a creek in the back.
A kidney-shaped pool silently longs for company.

I know nothing about the man whom I'm about to call.
Now, at least, I have the face of his house to look at.

I wait.

I walk the entire length of my living room twice.
I straighten out the rugs and untangle their fringes.

Then I pick up my phone from the dining-room table and punch in the number that's listed with Walter's address.

The phone beeps once, then twice, then three times.
I fend off a spell of nausea. I have to ask an invisible
stranger whether his father wrote a letter in defense of
my grandfather who was a member of the Nazi Party.
   Four times. What if he is someone else's son?
Five times. Someone whose family perished in the Holocaust?
Six times. How would someone like that react to the
cold call from a Nazi Party member's grandchild?

I stop counting. I just hope that Walter W. is not
in his house with the blue façade and the palm
tree and hot-pink blooming rosebush in the front.
A machine answers. Relieved, I wait for the beep and
remind myself to speak without a German accent.

8151.   SUNSET ON THE MIAMI RIVER, FLA.

"Hello, this is a message for Walter. I sent you a letter a couple of weeks ago. I'm looking for information about my grandfather —"

"Hello," a tired voice says on the other end. Walter has been listening all along.

"Hello. Did you ... hear my message?"

"Yes. And I received your letter as well."

I detect a faint German accent.

"I wasn't sure whether your letter was ... well, why don't you tell me what this is all about?"

He is interested enough not to have hung up yet, and so I begin with my confession to this stranger.

Google Street View confirms it's permanently sunny in Walter's
town in Florida. In Brooklyn, outside my frosted window,
my Caribbean next-door neighbor's ancient, faded-pink
plastic flamingos are being weighed down by heavily
falling snow. My backyard is white and perfect like
the surface of an egg, and none of the stray cats
dare disturb its purity.

Are there stray cats in Walter's town?

The longer
I talk to Walter about Willi,
the more uncomfortable I get.

The more uncomfortable I get,
the heavier my German accent becomes.

Maybe a flock of flamingos is passing by over Walter's
house at this moment. Perhaps a ripe coconut is
falling from the palm tree, landing wearily
on the crew-cut lawn
with a thud.

A sequence of quiet yeses on the other end
throughout my monologue confirms that
Walter W. is listening.    Then it is his turn to speak:

"The people you
are looking for —

yes, they were
my parents."

Suddenly, my house in Brooklyn and the one on Google Maps are directly connected, and when I zoom in, I can see a tiny patch of clover growing at the edge of the flower bed; I can see small patches of blotchy white lichen growing on the carefully coiffed jasmine tree in the front; I can see that a slightly tilted rosebush branch is gently propped up by a metal stake.

And now I can picture Walter, too, sitting on the sofa, propping the receiver against his slightly tilted head with the carefully coiffed white hair.

I have found the son of my grandfather's friend and I've forgotten all about my German accent.

"I didn't write back because I thought your letter might be part of a Social Security scam," Walter says. Now that he knows Willi's story, he's not afraid to tell me his own.

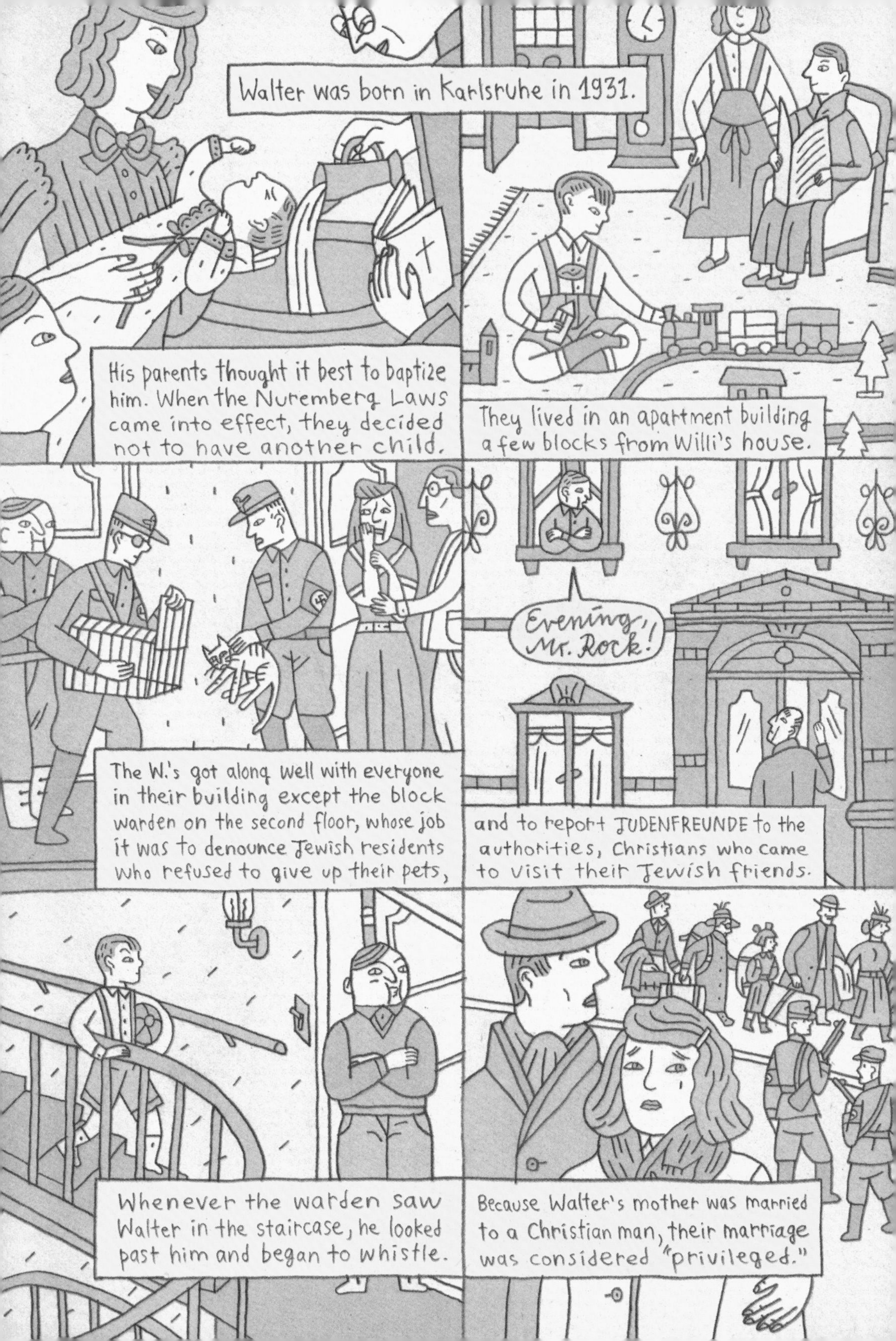
Walter was born in Karlsruhe in 1931.
His parents thought it best to baptize him. When the Nuremberg Laws came into effect, they decided not to have another child.
They lived in an apartment building a few blocks from Willi's house.
The W.'s got along well with everyone in their building except the block warden on the second floor, whose job it was to denounce Jewish residents who refused to give up their pets,
Evening, Mr. Rock!
and to report JUDENFREUNDE to the authorities, Christians who came to visit their Jewish friends.
Whenever the warden saw Walter in the staircase, he looked past him and began to whistle.
Because Walter's mother was married to a Christian man, their marriage was considered "privileged."

Thus they didn't have to relocate to a JUDENHAUS (Jew house), Selma didn't have to wear the Star of David, and she was spared from being sent to the camp in Gurs.

In 1944, thousands of Christian men married to Jewish women and "crossbreeds of the first and second degree" (Christians with one or two Jewish grandparents) were forced to join ORGANISATION TODT, a military unit named after its founder, Fritz Todt, originally composed of volunteers, and later also of concentration camp detainees, prisoners of war, forced laborers, and Germans rejected from military service. Some in the unit were sent to the most dangerous combat zones, to build fortifications and rocket-launching platforms.

"Everyone referred to this unit as 'Organisation Tod' — without the t," Walter says, "because most people never returned."

TOD is the German word for "death."

When Walter's father was summoned, he knew he wouldn't make it back alive. Terrified, he consulted his friend across the hall, who worked for the city's employment office.

"He told my father to eat a lot of sugar before his medical exam.

My father had diabetes, you see, and —"

Walter's voice breaks.

Somewhere in Florida, inside a blue house,
   a man is crying because he remembers a moment
      seventy years ago when a neighbor emerged as a true friend.

"— and when he had his exam, his sugar level was so high
   that he was declared unfit to work in the Todt unit."

"Did many people try to help you?"
"Yes, many. My father worked for a butcher, and when my mother
   was told she was going to be deported to Theresienstadt —"

"I am sorry if my questions are making you sad."
"That's OK. I sometimes get a little emotional," Walter says softly,
and beneath his English, I detect the southern-German intonation
                              I am so intimately familiar with.

"You must have loved your parents very much."
"Yes, I did. You see, my father did everything in his power
                  to protect her. And when he was old and ill,
                        she did the same for him."

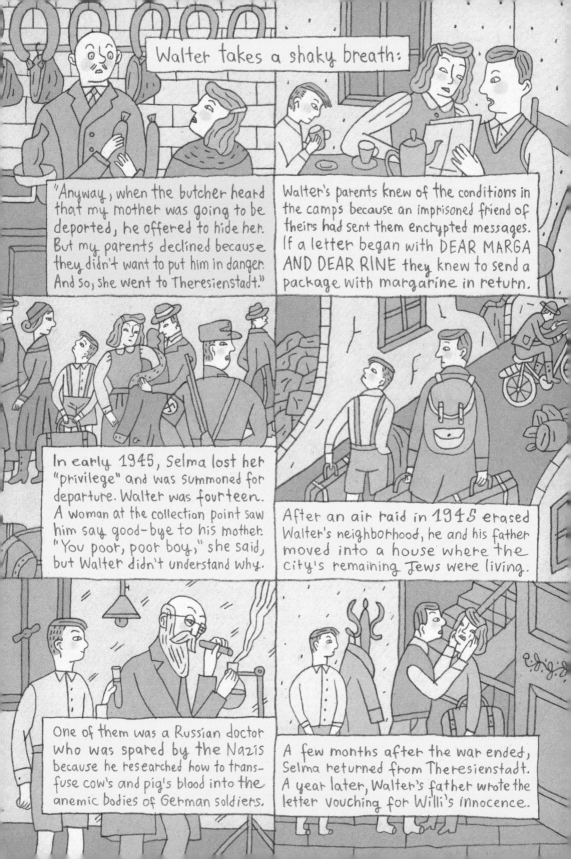

Walter takes a shaky breath:

"Anyway, when the butcher heard that my mother was going to be deported, he offered to hide her. But my parents declined because they didn't want to put him in danger. And so, she went to Theresienstadt."

Walter's parents knew of the conditions in the camps because an imprisoned friend of theirs had sent them encrypted messages. If a letter began with DEAR MARGA AND DEAR RINE they knew to send a package with margarine in return.

In early 1945, Selma lost her "privilege" and was summoned for departure. Walter was fourteen. A woman at the collection point saw him say good-bye to his mother. "You poor, poor boy," she said, but Walter didn't understand why.

After an air raid in 1945 erased Walter's neighborhood, he and his father moved into a house where the city's remaining Jews were living.

One of them was a Russian doctor who was spared by the Nazis because he researched how to transfuse cow's and pig's blood into the anemic bodies of German soldiers.

A few months after the war ended, Selma returned from Theresienstadt. A year later, Walter's father wrote the letter vouching for Willi's innocence.

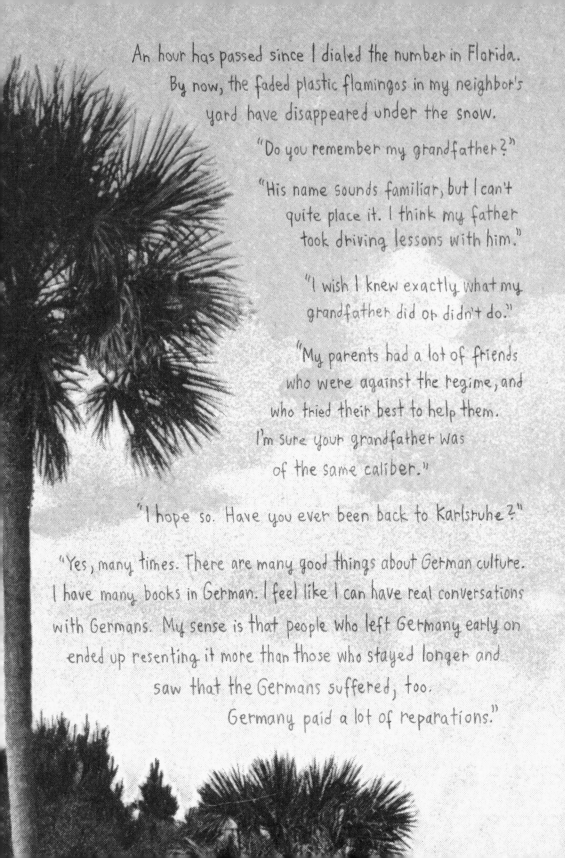

An hour has passed since I dialed the number in Florida. By now, the faded plastic flamingos in my neighbor's yard have disappeared under the snow.

"Do you remember my grandfather?"

"His name sounds familiar, but I can't quite place it. I think my father took driving lessons with him."

"I wish I knew exactly what my grandfather did or didn't do."

"My parents had a lot of friends who were against the regime, and who tried their best to help them. I'm sure your grandfather was of the same caliber."

"I hope so. Have you ever been back to Karlsruhe?"

"Yes, many times. There are many good things about German culture. I have many books in German. I feel like I can have real conversations with Germans. My sense is that people who left Germany early on ended up resenting it more than those who stayed longer and saw that the Germans suffered, too. Germany paid a lot of reparations."

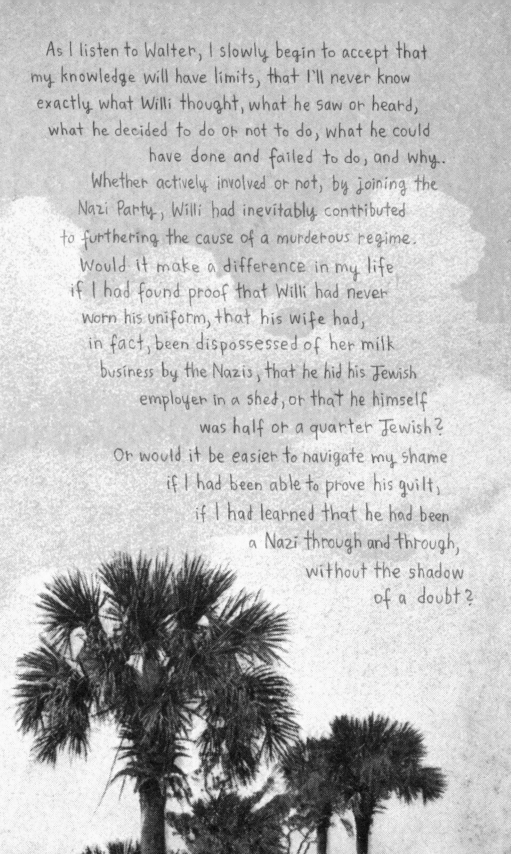

As I listen to Walter, I slowly begin to accept that
my knowledge will have limits, that I'll never know
exactly what Willi thought, what he saw or heard,
what he decided to do or not to do, what he could
have done and failed to do, and why.
Whether actively involved or not, by joining the
Nazi Party, Willi had inevitably contributed
to furthering the cause of a murderous regime.
Would it make a difference in my life
if I had found proof that Willi had never
worn his uniform, that his wife had,
in fact, been dispossessed of her milk
business by the Nazis, that he hid his Jewish
employer in a shed, or that he himself
was half or a quarter Jewish?
Or would it be easier to navigate my shame
if I had been able to prove his guilt,
if I had learned that he had been
a Nazi through and through,
without the shadow
of a doubt?

"You shouldn't feel guilty,"
Walter says with a soft tone
of voice, and by telling me this,
he does exactly
   what his father
      had once done for
         my grandfather:
he signs a testimonial for me.

And even though I know that I can't accept forgiveness for the
   unforgivable, that individual atonement can't erase the suffering
      of millions, the warmth of his voice and his generosity make me
         feel intimately bound to him, the way I had always longed
            to be bound to my own grandfather.

                                        "Thank you," I reply.

As I hang up the phone and look out the window,
    I see that it has stopped snowing.

I see a cat venture out of its hiding place.
    It lifts its paw and leaves the first print
        that breaks the perfect, blinding whiteness.

# 15.
# SHAKING
# HANDS

When I return to Külsheim this winter, crows have replaced skylarks, and snow has soundproofed the fields and forests.

A snowball lands on my winter coat.

My cousin Michael's youngest daughter laughs mischievously. "We have to make up for all of the snowball fights we missed out on over the years," her mother says, and I find myself having to fight back tears. We walk down the narrow path that leads to Annemarie's house. "Should I address her formally or informally?" I ask my cousin Iris.

"Funny. She asked me the same thing. I told her to use the informal form, of course."

By an unspoken agreement, I am at the front of the group.
My feet feel heavier with each step. I try to focus
on the path ahead of me until we've reached the house.
After all these years, I finally ring my aunt's bell.
The door opens immediately.

There she stands.

Small.

Delicate.

Short haired.

Sharp eyed.

Her half-curious, half-skeptical smile
makes me feel half-relieved at most.
She takes my hand and shakes it slowly.
"Let me look at you," she says, and doesn't let go.

"Let me look at you," she says again,
and I feel her hand shaking in mine.
Shaking like her mother Maria's hands
when she got older.

Shaking like my father's foot on the gas pedal.

Her gaze is as firm as her grip.
By the way she looks at me, I can tell that she is
searching my face for traces of my father.

Or is it my uncle whom she is looking for?

With my hand still clamped in hers, Annemarie takes me to a wall of family photographs. She points at one framed face after another and explains who's who.

"This is Maria, your grandmother."
She nods toward a photograph in a heavy golden frame.
Maria smiles. In her arms, she holds a newborn baby.

Her grandson. My brother.

Throughout the years of silence, this picture of my brother had hung on Annemarie's living-room wall.

But because Maria holds him facing toward her, all you can see of my brother is the back of his head.

This might be the only chance I'll ever have to ask Annemarie about what I've been burning to find out for so long. But something keeps me from mustering the courage.

As if she has read my mind, she says,
"Michael tells me you're writing a book about our family and the war, and that you have some questions?"

I feel equally relieved and terrified.
I present my questions, one by one,
and catalog her answers in my head.

**#1** Is it true that Alois was in prison because he spoke out against the Nazis?

No. He was locked up for three days because he had complained that he was being drafted at 40 years of age and kept away from tending to his farm.

**#2** What were his political views?

I don't know, but I remember that whenever Mr. Steinert's windows were open, my father kept his mouth shut.

**#3** Did Alois have Jewish friends?

He used to work with Jewish cattle dealers, and some of his classmates were Jewish.

**#4** Was he there when the incident at the fountain happened?

I have no idea, but I remember that he forbade me to leave the house that day.

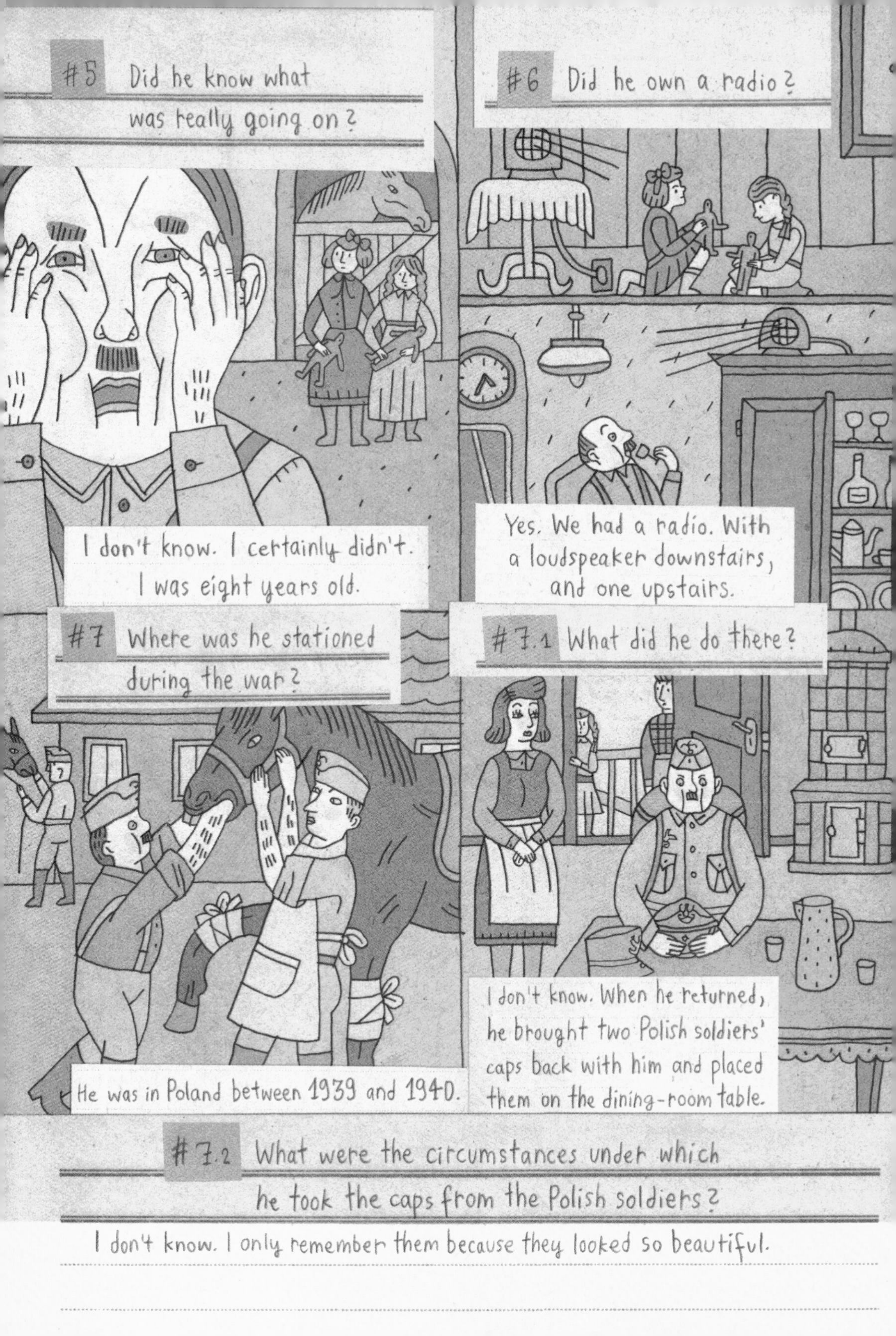

#5 Did he know what was really going on?
I don't know. I certainly didn't. I was eight years old.
#6 Did he own a radio?
Yes. We had a radio. With a loudspeaker downstairs, and one upstairs.
#7 Where was he stationed during the war?
He was in Poland between 1939 and 1940.
#7.1 What did he do there?
I don't know. When he returned, he brought two Polish soldiers' caps back with him and placed them on the dining-room table.
#7.2 What were the circumstances under which he took the caps from the Polish soldiers?
I don't know. I only remember them because they looked so beautiful.

As a teenager, I had imagined Annemarie's living room as modern and cold — spacious, with big floor-to-ceiling windows. I had pictured myself sitting across from her, pretending to be a stranger shooting a documentary about Külsheim. I had imagined talking in a confident, professional voice, and her looking at me with an expressionless face, showing no interest in my film.

And I had imagined her finally pushing a stack of photographs of my uncle across the living-room table — a large stack, given that my father had told me he only took a few photographs when he left.

In reality, everything is different. The house isn't cold. There are no floor-to-ceiling glass windows. I'm not pretending to be a stranger, and therefore, I don't sound confident. Her face isn't expressionless, and she is interested in my project.

In preparation for my visit, she collected my uncle's photographs, his letters from the front line, and his obituary and laid them out in neat piles on the table.

But instead of the large stack I had imagined, there are only a handful of photographs — because my father took most of them, she tells me.

"I haven't looked at any of this in a long time," she says.

Ach, es ist ja kaum zu faſſen,
Daß du nicht mehr kehrſt zurück,
So jung mußt du dein Leben laſſen,
Zerſtört iſt unſer ganzes Glück.
Du warſt ſo gut, du ſtarbſt ſo früh,
Du warſt uns alles, wir vergeſſen
   deiner nie.

Alas, it is unfathomable,
that you will not return,
that you have left us, oh so young,
now all our happiness is gone.
You were so good, you died so soon,
you meant everything to us,
we will remember you forever.

Annemarie's eyes turn shiny. She has created a paper shrine.
For my uncle. For me. And for herself.
She wants me to see everything.

Schmerzlich traf uns die traurige Nachricht vom Heldentod unseres lieben, einzigen, edlen Sohnes und Bruders

# Franz Karl Krug

Er gab sein junges Leben von kaum 18 Jahren in treuer Pflichterfüllung am 19. Juli 1944, an der Südfront, für seine geliebte Heimat.

In tiefem Herzeleid:

## Alois Krug u. Frau Maria

The sad news of the heroic death of our dear, only, precious son and brother Franz-karl Krug has left us with great pain. Hardly 18 years old, he gave his young life to his beloved HEIMAT on July 19, 1944, while loyally performing his duty at the Southern front. With deep sorrow:
Alois Krug and wife Maria (born Geier),
little daughter Annemarie, and family.

"We once visited his grave in Italy."
"We did once, too," I say.

"I'm sweating. It's nervousness," she says,
and picks up one of the photo albums.

As we look at the photographs together,
big Franz-Karl's life rises up once more in front of us.

And in our silence,
for one moment,

we are a perfectly united family.

*Ein kleines Andenken*

"A little souvenir," Franz-Karl wrote on the back of the last photo he sent from Italy in January 1944, the last one that exists of him. "Didn't come out well, though. Will have pictures snapped again soon, hope that those will turn out better."

Witnessing the change in his appearance is painful. The softness in his face has gone.

It's been decades since she last read any of Franz-Karl's letters, Annemarie tells me. I pick up one of them, dated May 7, 1944.

"We aren't in the land of the hypocritical dagos any longer. The people here are very, very friendly. On the first day, the women came and wanted to wash our laundry.

They bring us everything. White bread and bacon, beer, milk. The beer is first-class here, too, but it's expensive. Two pengő per liter...

Your goslings are probably already grown up by now, eh? There are lots of them here. We leave at 7 or 7:30 in the mornings and return home with them in the evenings. They have their old ones walking with them. Today I counted 43 in one batch with 5 old ones.

...P.S.: Today we were at the movies. A first-class film: HAB MICH LIEB."

HAB MICH LIEB. Please Love Me. I want to watch this film, and finally see exactly what my uncle saw.

Another letter, dated July 12, 1944,
was written four days before Franz-Karl's death:

"If I write to you more infrequently these days, please don't
be afraid. I don't have that many occasions to write anymore.
One is glad when one can rest a little. With a thousand
greetings and kisses I remain your son Franz-Karl!
Until a happy reunion! Special regards to Annemarie."

"He wrote to us three times a week from Italy," Annemarie tells me, and it sounds as if she's waiting for more letters to come.

"What were his letters like?"
"I think he was homesick."

"And what was he like?"
"He was diligent. Cheerful. Humane."
Franz-Karl is still her big brother. Her real brother.

"How did he feel about the war?"
"Listen, young lady, he was seventeen when he was drafted and eighteen when he was killed!"

"Do you remember the moment when the letter announcing his death arrived?"
"Of course I remember. I was out in the yard, playing with my friends. We were thinking about what to make for dessert at my birthday party."

"It must have been very hard for you."
"Well. We never made a dessert after all."

"You can have that."
    Annemarie hands me a copy
        of Franz-Karl's obituary.

            Suddenly, her voice turns sour.
                "And that one, too!"
    She points at a photo of her and my father as children,
sitting together on a sled, surrounded by nothing but snow.

    "Are you sure?" I ask.
    "I don't need it anymore," she says firmly,
            and her smile makes me uncomfortable.

What would Annemarie and my father's relationship
be like if my uncle hadn't died in the war?

What would it be like
_____

if big Franz-Karl —
_____

the GOOD Franz-Karl, as his mother
had described him; the "dear, only,
precious son and brother," as his
obituary had referred to him, who
"meant everything to us" and who
"gave his young life to his beloved
HEIMAT"; the one who had promised
in his letter to "remain your son
Franz-Karl! Until a happy reunion!";
the son Maria had shed tears over
in the photograph in the article of the
NEUE BERLINER ILLUSTRIERTE, the
only son mentioned in it — "she lost
her son in the last war" — even
though she had brought a second one
into the world over a decade before

the article was written; the one who had been his father's
biological son without a doubt, the one who would have

looked after the farm, unlike his younger brother;
the one who shared Annemarie's shame when their
 mother went off with the soldiers to
Vienna, and who, had he still been alive,
would have shared Annemarie's shame
as well when rumors were spread about
the man in the backyard who dyed
uniforms black, and when Maria was
condemned from the pulpit by Külsheim's
priest because she'd joined the Jehovah's
Witnesses; her big brother who would
have been there to protect Annemarie
all her life if only he hadn't died in the
last World War; the Franz-Karl who
both separates my aunt and me and
inextricably binds us together

— what would it be like if he
were sitting in the living room with us right now?

Who would we be as a family
if the war had never happened?

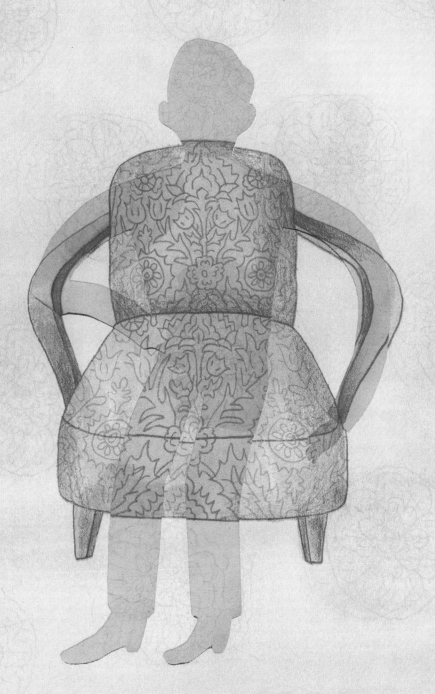

"Look, look," Annemarie says,
as we all sit around the dining-room table and eat.
"You're left-handed! I am left-handed, too.
But I was forced to write with my right."

With her shaking left hand,
Annemarie raises her glass.

And as the wine from the grapes of the family vineyard
flows from my mouth to my stomach and then into my veins,
I know that each step that leads me closer to my uncle,
each new word that's added to my family narrative
entangles me, that I am irrevocably intertwined
with people and with places,
with stories and with histories.

"To left-handedness, to brothers dead and alive,
to shaking feet and hands,
to the unescapability of who we are,"
I think, and raise my glass.

This is the closest I have ever been to my uncle.

And this is the closest I will ever get.

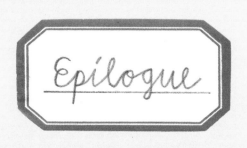

# Epilogue

One year later, my husband orders a box full of Leitz binders on the Internet "because they'll make you feel secure," he says.

. . .

My mother makes  me a pillow out of my grandmother Maria's monogrammed dowry linen and offers me one of the cast-iron pans with which my great-grandmother warmed up noodles at the Rose. "It's my best pan. Nothing ever sticks," she says.

. . .

Plans are made to restore Külsheim's old mikvah, and a memorial stone is erected where the synagogue used to be, "as a manifestation of sadness and shame," Külsheim's new mayor says on the day it is installed.

. . .

My father returns to Külsheim and walks around the town, "to see how it has developed." He meets Michael and Iris, his nephew and niece, whom he hasn't seen since they were children, and he visits the old farmhouse where he grew up.

    "Do you want to see your sister?" I ask.

    "I have no reason to ever see her again."

He goes back to the green patch of land he owns, "not for sentimental reasons, but to visualize where it is located, exactly." "Have you ever thought of selling it," I ask. "No, it's best not to sell it. Land is gaining in value. Chinese investors are beginning to buy vineyards in the region. And you'll inherit it one day."

On the phone from Brooklyn I ask my mother, "Next time you go, can you bring a handful of earth for me?"
"Yes, we can do that, if you want."

. . .

While going through my grandfather Willi's old photographs in the shoebox again, I find one that I hadn't noticed before: It is the photograph showing the arrival of the Jewish lawyer Ludwig Marum and the other Social Democrats at Kislau concentration camp, soon after they were paraded through the streets of Karlsruhe — the same photograph that I had seen at the archive in Karlsruhe. But because of the way the people in it are positioned, I can tell that Willi's copy was taken one or two seconds after the one I had found at the archive. Why did Willi own this photo, an original print of an event orchestrated by the Nazis to taunt and intimidate? A stamp on the back reveals that it was developed by a photo studio in a small town near the camp. Such a small studio could have never printed enough copies to be used for large-scale propaganda purposes. Why, then, was Willi given one?

I apply for American citizenship and in the naturalization form am asked to answer the same question Willi answered in his 1946 US military questionnaire:

"Between March 23, 1933, and May 8, 1945, did you work for or associate in any way with the Nazi government of Germany?"

I check the box on the right, knowing that my grandfather would have checked the one on the left, and I'm glad that I asked all the questions I needed to ask — that I went back and collected the bread crumbs, that I kept looking until I was sure that none were left, that I know now what I didn't know before:

that HEIMAT can only be found again in memory, that it is something that only begins to exist once you've lost it.

'''

The 2017 national election in Germany has given rise to a new right-wing party. The extreme right has claimed seats in parliament again, for the first time in more than half a century.

'''

Standing in a crowded New York City subway car, I remember the letter the mayor of Karlsruhe wrote to the police chief in 1940:

"Constant complaints have been made about the fact that local Jews have been behaving brashly and provocatively in crowded tram cars and have refused to give up their seats for German women."

A man in a yarmulke standing next to me asks the woman sitting in front of me to offer me her seat, and I thank him, still uncomfortable with my German accent. He can tell by the shape of my belly that something is growing in there, something with no consciousness. Someone with a state of mind as pure and undisturbed as the surface of freshly fallen snow.

Uhu was invented by a German pharmacist as the first synthetic (bone-glue-free) resin adhesive in the world, in 1932. Because at the time stationery products were commonly named after birds, the new adhesive was named Uhu, after the eagle-owl, a bird native to the Black Forest, where the glue's founder was from. The adhesive, also referred to as ALLESKLEBER (everything-glue), became known for being able to glue together materials of any kind. Uhu made it into GUINNESS WORLD RECORDS for using only 9 drops to glue together two steel cylinders that connected a crane hook with a pickup truck. During WWII, Uhu's ads declared model making as KRIEGSWICHTIG (war-important), and Uhu became popular with children for assembling miniature military vehicles. After the war, Uhu became an integral part of Germany's do-it-yourself, zero-waste mentality. Today, I use imported Uhu to repair the soles of my worn shoes, broken chinaware, to fix peeling wallpaper and objects that are brittle and have been glued together many times before. Even though Uhu is the strongest glue available, it cannot cover up the crack.

# Selected Sources

Historical information and eyewitness accounts from Külsheim were based on interviews conducted with the town's residents, and on the book GESCHICHTE DER BRUNNENSTADT KÜLSHEIM (Stadtverwaltung Külsheim, 1992), by Irmtraut Edelmann, Helmuth Lauf, and Elmar Weiss.

Historical information and eyewitness accounts from Karlsruhe were taken from the books KARLSRUHE 1945 (Braun, 1986) and HAKENKREUZ UND JUDENSTERN (Badenia, 1988), by Josef Werner; LE GAULEITER WAGNER: LE BOURREAU DE L'ALSACE (La Nuée Bleue, 2011), by Jean-Laurent Vonau; ". . . SIE HATTEN NOCH DIE FRECHHEIT ZU WEINEN . . ." (Gewerkschaft Erziehung und Wissenschaft Bezirk Nordbaden, 1979), by Peter Baumbusch, Heide and Manfred Czerni, Dagmar Dengler, Heinz-Günther Klusch, Helmut Kranz, Horst Sommer, and Günter Wimmer; and ZIELORT KARLSRUHE (Regionalkultur, 2005), by Erich Lacker, my 7th-grade chemistry teacher, who I knew little about as a student, and whose book about the Allied bombings of Karlsruhe I discovered only by chance at the New York Public Library during the research for this memoir.

Additional historical facts were taken from HITLER'S JEWISH SOLDIERS (University Press of Kansas, 2002), by Bryan Mark Rigg; ON THE NATURAL HISTORY OF DESTRUCTION (Hamish Hamilton/Penguin Books, 1999), by W. G. Sebald; and THE HISTORY OF THE GERMAN RESISTANCE, 1933–1945 (McGill–Queen's University Press, 1996), by Peter Hoffmann. Historical facts were checked by Kat Rickard and Jonas Wegerer.

Quotes were taken from the above-mentioned publications, as well as from YOUR JOB IN GERMANY (United States War Department, 1945); the United States Citizenship and Immigration Services application form N-400; BROCKHAUS. DIE ENZYKLOPÄDIE IN 24 BÄNDEN (Wissen Media, 1996–1999); DEUTSCHES WÖRTERBUCH (Weidmann, 1854), by Jacob and Wilhelm Grimm; NEUES LEBEN (Bassermann, 1851–1852), by Berthold Auerbach; JOSEPH GOEBBELS TAGEBÜCHER (Piper, 1992), edited by Ralf Georg Reuth; DAS LETZTE JAHR IN BRIEFEN (Loeper, 2016), by Andreé Fischer-Marum; and from Adolf Hitler speeches quoted in JUGEND IM DRITTEN REICH. DIE HITLER-JUGEND UND IHRE GEGNER (Diederichs, 1982), by Arno Klönne, and THE SPEECHES OF ADOLF HITLER: APRIL 1922—AUGUST 1939 (Oxford University Press, 1942), edited by Norman Hepburn Baynes. The German lyrics to the 1931 song "Cikánka" ("You Black Gypsy"), by the Bohemian military musician and composer Karel Vacek, were written by the Austrian lyricist and writer Fritz Löhner-Beda, who was murdered in Auschwitz in 1942. Löhner-Beda was also the co-composer of "Das Buchenwaldlied" ("The Buchenwald Song"), which is known as the concentration camp's anthem. Additional quotes were taken online from: http://www.transodra-online.net, https://forum.axishistory.com, and http://www.nytimes.com.

Photographs of the German population's forced confrontation with the atrocities committed by the Nazis in concentration camps were published with permission of the United States Holocaust Memorial Museum. The views or opinions expressed in this book and the context in which the images are used, do not necessarily reflect the views or policy of, nor imply approval or endorsement by, the United States Holocaust Memorial Museum. The photograph of Julius Hirsch was provided by Wikimedia Commons. Portraits of female concentration camp guards were either in the public domain and provided by Wikimedia Commons or published with the permission of the Imperial War Museum (BU 9682). The photograph of the destroyed city of Karlsruhe in Chapter 1 was published courtesy of Stadtarchiv Karlsruhe (8/Alben 412/11). Additional historical photographs were in the public domain and provided by Florida International University and the New York Public Library. Archival materials in Chapter 9 were reproduced with the permission of the Stadtarchiv Külsheim, Archivverbund Main-Tauber, and included the documents StAWt-K G 10 A 776 and A 933, K-G10 A776. Willi Rock's US military file (465 h Nr. 11214) was reproduced with permission from the Generallandesarchiv Karlsruhe. The article "Bitten und beten zwecklos" was taken from the NEUE BERLINER ILLUSTRIERTE, issue number 16/1960. The article that was written in response was published in FRÄNKISCHE NACHRICHTEN on May 4, 1960. Photographs of my uncle Franz-Karl that are not in my father's possession were kindly provided by my aunt Annemarie. All objects, letters, and photographs in the SCRAPBOOK OF A MEMORY ARCHIVIST were found at German flea markets and household liquidation shops. Their original owners could not be traced.

My uncle Franz-Karl's date of death was erroneously stated in his obituary as July 19, 1944. The date should have read July 16, 1944, instead.

# Acknowledgments

I'm deeply grateful to my parents, Rita and Franz Krug, to my brother, Lasse, and my aunt Karin Rock for their unconditional love and unwavering belief in me, and for their bravery in letting me ask those questions about our family that had never been asked before; to my cousins and to the wife of my father's cousin for their openness, and to my father's sister for meeting me and for sharing her memory of Uncle Franz-Karl; and to Simone Dollmann for her enduring friendship, advice, and encouragement.

I am indebted to Elyse Cheney of The Cheney Agency for believing in my book and taking me on as one of her authors, and to my agent, Alex Jacobs — the best agent I could have ever hoped for — for his kindness, his tireless support and guidance, for reassuring me and repeatedly untangling my frazzled mind; to my US publisher, Nan Graham, and my German publisher, Wolfgang Ferchl, for their immediate and continuous enthusiasm; to my US editors, Kathy Belden and Liese Mayer, my German editors, Britta Egetemeier and Angelika Schedel, and my UK editor, Helen Conford, for their trust and their hard work in helping me shape endless amounts of material into a consistent narrative.

I want to thank the John Simon Guggenheim Memorial Foundation, the Pollock-Krasner Foundation, and the Maurice Sendak Foundation for supporting this project, and I am especially grateful to Lynn Caponera and Dona McAdams of the Maurice Sendak Foundation for their warmth and generosity.

I'd like to express my gratitude to all those at The New School who granted me the time needed to develop this project, and in particular to Deans Nadine Bourgeois, Anne Gaines, and Joel Towers; and to Mei Kanamoto, Sam Li, Luis Nazario, Maria Theresa Putri, Alicia Raines, Kat Rickard, and Jessica Zuniga for their assisting me with this project, especially for the countless hours spent fixing each typo by hand. (I shall be held accountable for the ones that still made it into this book.)

I am also thankful for the support of the following people:

Jonathan Bach, Alfred Bauch, James Baumann, Harry Bliss, Marzia and Maurizio Corraini, Dave Eggers, Renate Evers, the GABY GLÜCKSELIG STAMMTISCH, Karen Green, Vicky Hattam, Steve Heller, Sally Howe, Ben Katchor, Brad Kessler, Carin Kuoni, Catherine Lutz, Brian McMullen, Marion Moran, Mick Moran, Françoise Mouly, Eileen Pollack, Lauren Redniss, Susanne Rock, Shoaib Rokadiya, Jeff Roth, Alanah Roy, David and Joni Sandlin, Claus-Dieter Schmidt, Oliver Schmitt, Niels Schröder, Jürgen Schuhladen-Krämer, Gershom Schwalfenberg, David Seldner, Teresa Shelley, Otto Spengler, Michael Spudic, Margaret Stead, the SÜTTERLINSTUBE HAMBURG, Sara Varon, Carola Väth, Werner Wunsch, and Susan Yelavich.

Most important, I thank Steven Guarnaccia for never tiring of reading through my latest edits, for continuously reminding me in the middle of the night that I will eventually finish this memoir, for his inspiration, devotion, and reassurance, and for spending his life with me; and our daughter (one of whose first sentences was "Mama work book") for being in my life.

## About the Author

Nora Krug's drawings and visual narratives have appeared in publications such as THE NEW YORK TIMES, THE GUARDIAN, and LE MONDE DIPLOMATIQUE. Her short-form graphic biography "Kamikaze," about a surviving Japanese WWII pilot, was included in the 2012 editions of THE BEST AMERICAN COMICS and THE BEST AMERICAN NONREQUIRED READING.

Her animations were shown at Sundance, and she is the recipient of fellowships from the Maurice Sendak Foundation, Fulbright, the John Simon Guggenheim Memorial Foundation, the Pollock-Krasner Foundation, and of medals from the Society of Illustrators and the Art Directors Club of New York.

She is an associate professor in the illustration program at Parsons School of Design in New York and lives in Brooklyn with her family.

Willi, Aunt Karin, my brother, and me, 1984

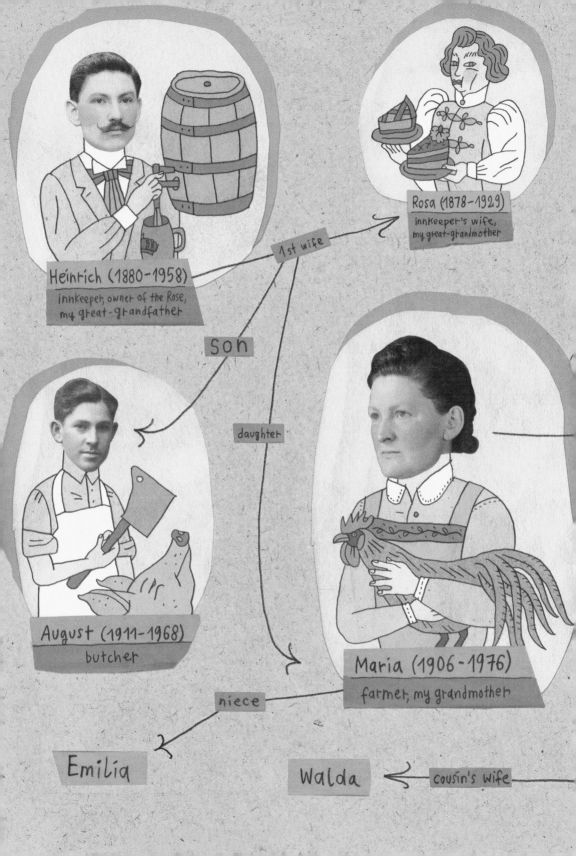

Heinrich (1880–1958)
innkeeper, owner of the Rose,
my great-grandfather

1st wife

Rosa (1878–1929)
innkeeper's wife,
my great-grandmother

Son

daughter

August (1911–1968)
butcher

Maria (1906–1976)
farmer, my grandmother

niece

Emilia

Walda

cousin's wife